The New Forest Companion

A WALKER'S GUIDE

ANNE-MARIE EDWARDS

COUNTRYSIDE BOOKS
NEWBURY BERKSHIRE

First published 2005

© Anne-Marie Edwards 2005

All rights reserved.
No reproduction permitted without the prior
permission of the publisher:

COUNTRYSIDE BOOKS
3 Catherine Road
Newbury, Berkshire

To view our complete range of books,
please visit us at
www.countrysidebooks.co.uk

ISBN 1 85306 907 8

Photographs by Mike Edwards

Illustrations by Louise Burston

Produced through MRM Associates Ltd., Reading
Printed by Arrowsmith, Bristol

Contents

Location of the Walks

ABOUT THE FOREST

The New Forest in Hampshire is one of the most beautiful areas of countryside in Britain. In 2005 its beauty and unique character was recognised by the Government and it was created a National Park. But the New Forest is a National Park with a difference! It is a medieval hunting forest with its own history and customs which by some miracle has survived into our own times. It owes its origin to William the Conqueror who in 1079 declared the wild country near his capital Winchester, stretching from Southampton Water west to the Avon valley and from the Wiltshire Downs south to the Solent, his own special hunting ground. No-one could farm in his 'new' Forest or disturb the deer which were his own preserve. Harsh laws were enacted to make sure his commands were carried out.

Of course encroachments have been made over the centuries and the New Forest boundaries are not as extensive, but over 100 square miles of medieval forest remain, criss-crossed by a multitude of tracks dipping over river valleys and heathland and leading beneath the shade of great oak and beech woods which provided timber for Britain's 'wooden walls'. The oldest woods, termed by the Forestry Commission 'ancient and ornamental', are carefully preserved. Many of the trees have been cut short, or pollarded at an early period of growth. As this custom was declared illegal in 1698, they must be over 400 years old. Without

their heads, their main trunks have sprouted several stems which now, wreathed with ivy and often set with little gardens of ferns, spread massive arms over the Forest floor. One of the rambles in this book takes you to the oldest oak tree of all, the Knightwood oak, through glades of mighty trees, the home of the Purple Emperor butterfly and the wild gladiolus. All wild creatures love these woods. You will see fallow deer with their branching antlers, the smaller reddish-brown roe, the small spotted sika, and, if you are lucky, a red deer stag guarding his harem of hinds with their floppy ears and large eloquent eyes. Badgers and foxes follow their own tracks through the undergrowth. And you will gather a host of unforgettable impressions – out on the heath, larks soaring and singing even on grey days, heather and gorse smelling as rich as honey, the velvet green of the Forest lawn, a leggy foal nuzzling his mother for comfort in a world too new for him.

But nature is only part of the Forest's story. In order to survive the people who lived close to the Forest had to be granted certain rights. Gradually the harsh laws were relaxed to allow them to pasture ponies, cattle, donkeys and geese in the Forest and, during the pannage season in autumn, when the acorns and beech seeds (mast) had fallen, they could turn out their pigs to enjoy a feast. Other rights included permission to gather firewood 'by hook or by crook', cut peat and spread marl dug from pits in the

Forest to improve the quality of their land. These rights are attached to certain houses and today their occupants, the commoners, exercise their rights as vigorously as ever. They own the famous ponies, a breed only found in the New Forest, rounding them up at various times of the year for marking and sale with scenes reminiscent of the Wild West. For these tough, shaggy ponies have not forgotten their wild ancestry and will head for cover the moment they suspect their freedom is threatened. Their tempers are uncertain and it is dangerous to feed them, however appealing they look.

As you walk away from the crowded centres, you will find that the Forest is a quiet place, possibly quieter than at any other time in its long history. In the past you would have met people who lived and worked here, all dependent to some extent on the Forest: gypsies, charcoal-burners, woodcutters, snake-catchers, swineherds, perhaps even smugglers as they led their ponies laden with contraband along its leafy ways. They may have gone, but the Forest holds their story still.

The walks in this book do not follow frequented routes. They are my own favourite walks, each of them revealing different aspects of the Forest's scenery and history. We follow a ridgeway deep into the great woods around Lyndhurst and take a smugglers' track to an Iron Age hill fort near Burley. We visit Canterton Glen where a stone marks the spot where, according to Forest tradition, William the Conqueror's favourite son, William Rufus fell from his horse with an arrow through his heart. We explore 'Churchplace' near Ashurst – one of several in the Forest – possibly the site of a Saxon village destroyed by William when he made the area his own hunting ground, and look at the origin of Woodgreen's 'Merry Sundays'. And as we follow Bishop's Dyke we wonder why a medieval bishop should wish to own a part of Forest marshland!

By custom, we are allowed to wander almost at will in the Forest. For the walker this is of course a blessing but it can give rise to some problems! There are few signposts as rights-of-way do not need to be indicated and there is a labyrinth of paths. (You will find signposts in some privately owned areas such as the Beaulieu Estate, and the Forest's designation as a National Park may result in some changes in the future.)

So I have planned this book as a series of safe circular walks. Most of the starting points are accessible by public transport as well as by car. South West Trains and Connex all stop in the Forest. For information tel: 08457 484950. Bus and coach services are provided by Wiltshire. and Dorset. For information tel: 01202 673555. National Express also runs services in this area. The sketch maps in the book are meant only as a general guide to the route and it is wise to walk with a map that shows the whole area. You may like to arm yourself with the Ordnance Survey Outdoor Leisure Map, No 22. The scale is ideal, 1:25 000 (4 cm to 1 km or about $2\frac{1}{2}$ inches to 1 mile). It is a large map but if you buy a plastic case to put it in it won't flap about in windy weather. However, Forest paths occasionally defeat even the map makers so it is a good idea to carry a compass. I prefer the Silva compass recommended by rambling associations which is small, light and easy to use. It is accompanied by a leaflet which explains in detail how to use it. However dry the Forest may appear there is sure to be a boggy path lurking somewhere so wear strong waterproof shoes or boots. I usually try to remember to carry some sticking plasters to use at the first hint of a blister which can ruin the most delightful of walks! The Forest is well supplied with excellent pubs and cafés, some of which

I mention but even if you do not plan a full-scale picnic, it is wise to carry a drink and a supply of sustaining food on all Forest expeditions. My family's usual lifesavers include fruit and nut bars, chocolate, fruit cake – the richer the better – and apples. I have found from first-hand experience that Forest bogs, identifiable by waving tufts of white cotton grass, are best avoided even if it means a detour. If you are in doubt keep to the heather, or ground under trees and look for animal tracks round the boggy area; deer don't like getting their feet wet. There is no need to worry about snakes. There are adders (with V-markings down their backs) whose bites are venomous but they are much more terrified of you than you are of them and will quickly get out of your way. However, if you are unfortunate enough to be bitten it is important to keep calm. Wash the bite if possible and go to the Accident and Emergency Department at either Southampton or Bournemouth Hospital where anti-snake serum is kept.

I hope you will try these walks and enjoy this lovely National Park. You will never tire of the New Forest. With its changing colours, its hazy shimmering distances, its dappled effects of light and shade, it is never the same from one day to the next. The Forest remains a continually unfolding source of delight.

Anne-Marie Edwards

Anne-Marie and her photographer husband in Bushy Bratley wood.

LYNDHURST

There is no better way to introduce yourself to the New Forest than to spend some time exploring the Forest's ancient administrative capital, Lyndhurst. To appreciate Lyndhurst you must approach the village on foot through the Forest. Come from the west through the hamlet of Bank or from the east making for the tree-crowned hill of Bolton's Bench and your first impression will be the right one – a lonely church spire encircled by trees. As you come closer, using the spire as your guide, even today it is easy to imagine the village as it must have looked to the traveller in times past: a cluster of friendly lights in the centre of a beautiful but inhospitable wilderness.

New Forest churches serve as landmarks and Lyndhurst's parish church of St Michael and All Angels stands at a high point in the village overlooking the main street. The fine east window was designed by the Pre-Raphaelite artist, Burne-Jones. In the churchyard is the grave of Mrs Hargreaves, the 'Alice' of Lewis Carroll's *Alice in Wonderland*. The Queen's House stands next to the church. Saxon monarchs hunted in this area and there has been a royal manor here since the 10th century. The present elegant house was largely rebuilt by Charles II. Under the same roof is the Verderers' Court dating from the 14th century. In Norman times the Verderers had to administer the terribly harsh Forest laws and the court still meets today to settle the claims and disputes of the commoners. Facing the courtroom is one of Lyndhurst's old 17th-century coaching inns, the Crown. Adjoining the car park where we begin this walk is the excellent New Forest Museum and Visitor Centre giving a richly rewarding insight into all aspects of Forest life.

PONDHEAD INCLOSURE AND BOLTON'S BENCH

Length: 2 miles

Approaching Lyndhurst from the east.

Starting point: Lyndhurst Central car park (GR 300 081). **Public Transport:** Lyndhurst is well served by buses. **Map:** Ordnance Survey Outdoor Leisure 22. **Refreshments:** Cafés, pubs and restaurants in the village.

This is an easy leisurely stroll suitable for everyone. There is a good, well-drained path all the way round – level enough for pushchairs – so it is ideal if you have small children or older people in your group. You will be surprised how much of the Forest's varied scenery of oak and beech woods and open heathland you can enjoy with very little effort! And, as always in the Forest, you will find that even a short walk will reveal interesting aspects of the Forest's story.

THE WALK

1 To start the walk do not take either of the routes leading from the car park to Lyndhurst High Street but walk past the No Entry signs and the side of the Visitor Centre along the lane that leads you to the A337, the Lyndhurst–Lymington road. When you reach the road turn right and follow the road in the direction of Lymington. You come to a grassy area, Goose Green. Cross the road ahead and walk straight over the Green. Cross to the pavement beside the Lymington Road and keep on in the direction of Lymington. You pass a phone box on your left then come to a minor road, Beechen Lane, on your left. It is opposite the drive leading to Foxlease House, the Girl Guides Association Training Centre.

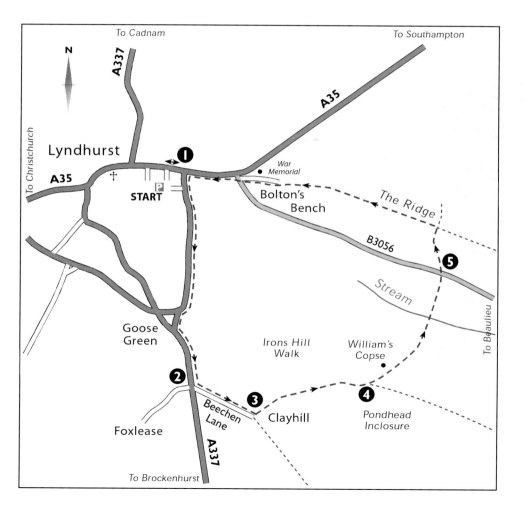

❷ Turn left down Beechen Lane and ahead you will see the tall oaks and beeches of Pondhead Inclosure. As you approach the inclosure you will see gates ahead with tall wire deer fences.

❸ Turn left through the left-hand gate and continue along a delightful woodland path.

Now, after only about ten minutes' walk, you are really in the Forest. The path is shaded by oaks and beeches, their ivy-darkened trunks rising from the dense thickets of holly which have protected them from browsing animals. Through the trees on your left you will glimpse Lyndhurst church spire.

Follow the path as it leads between Irons Hill Walk and Clayhill. The path bears right to take you into Pondhead Inclosure and then divides.

❹ Take the left-hand path.

After about 100 yards look carefully to the left of the path for an interesting memorial. In 1979 the New Forest celebrated 900 years as a Royal Forest. You will see a plaque on a hollowed wooden support in front of a special area designated 'William's Copse'. The plaque reads 'Nine hundred Sessile Oaks were planted here in 1979 to commemorate the creation of the New Forest by William I in 1079. May it contribute to the sylvan pleasures of our successors.'

The path crosses a wooden bridge over a stream and leads through a gate. Continue

Trees crown Bolton's Bench which is probably an ancient earthwork. It is named after Lord Bolton, Lord Warden of the Forest in 1688.

The memorial in Pondhead Inclosure commemorating 900 years of the Forest's history.

along the path to another gate (usually chained) beside a narrow wooden-railed walkway. After negotiating the walkway keep straight ahead to the minor road running from Lyndhurst to Beaulieu. Go over the road to the path ahead leading past a Forestry Commission barrier. Take the path which rises to lead you high on the heath to the east of Lyndhurst.

❺ Follow the path to a crossing path and turn left in the direction of Lyndhurst church spire.

You are now walking along The Ridge. This marks the boundary of an area enclosed as a deer park in 1291. From this vantage point you have wide views over the Forest heathlands, especially eastwards to the great 'ancient and ornamental' woods of Matley and Denny.

Continue along The Ridge and soon you will see the mound topped with a clump of trees known as Bolton's Bench rising a little to your left. This earthwork possibly dates back to the Iron Age and is named after Lord Bolton who was Lord Warden of the Forest in 1688. Pass Bolton's Bench on your left and the War Memorial on your right. The path becomes metalled and brings you down to the foot of Lyndhurst High Street. Walk up the High Street and turn left down the A337 Lyndhurst –Lymington road. The entry to the car park is the first lane on the right.

LYNDHURST TO ASHURST: A WALKER'S WAY

Length: 7 miles

The Beaulieu river flowing through Longwater Lawn.

Starting point: Lyndhurst Central car park (GR 300 081). **Public Transport:** Buses run to Lyndhurst and Ashurst, and trains to Ashurst Station. **Map:** Ordnance Survey Outdoor Leisure 22. This walk can easily be divided into two by making use of the bus service between Lyndhurst and Ashurst. **Refreshments:** Cafés, pubs and restaurants in both villages. **Campsite:** Ashurst. This village is the half-way point so the circular walk can be started here.

The great historian of the Forest, John Wise, wrote in his book *The New Forest*, first published in 1883, that the people of Lyndhurst 'ought to be the happiest and most contented in England, for they possess a wider park and nobler trees than even Royalty'. He could say the same today although if you arrive in the bustling Forest capital during a busy summer weekend you might find this difficult to believe! However, a few minutes' walk away the quiet glades and soft green lawns of the Forest are waiting for you to discover them. This circular walk from Lyndhurst to Ashurst and back will take you through some of the loveliest and most peaceful parts of the Forest.

THE WALK

❶ From the car park in Lyndhurst take either of the exits that lead to the High Street. Turn left up the hill towards the church but before you get there turn right at the traffic lights down Romsey Road. Continue past the road 'Racecourse View', and the sign for Pikes Hill and about 50 yards further on turn right to step over a stile to the edge of the golf course.

❷ Turn left, and keeping the railings close on your left, walk along the edge of the golf course until you come to a thick belt of trees. Turn right to follow the northern edge of the golf course with the trees on your left. Continue over a track which leads left through the trees to a bridge and keep on along the edge of the golf course until you come to the next track on the left which also leads to a bridge. This is our way. To make certain look right and you will see the spire of Lyndhurst church directly in line with our path.

❸ Turn left, cross the bridge, and follow the path ahead for a few yards to a crossing path. Turn right to a wide green path, part of the former racecourse.

❹ Bear left for a few yards along the path which bears right to head east through the woods. This is a beautiful walk shaded by ancient pollarded trees which spread their massive branches almost horizontally above the Forest floor.

❺ When you come to a wide crosstrack look right and you will see a gate leading to the main A35. Go straight over, go through a gate and follow the green path ahead. Leave some wooden buildings near Lodgehill Cottage on your right. Ignore the first main track on your left which leads to a Forestry Commission barrier and continue for a few more yards to a gravel crosstrack.

❻ Turn left and follow the gravel track as it climbs slightly uphill. At the top, by a ramp, keep straight on over a crossing track, to follow a gravel track downhill. Go straight over the next crossing track. Keep straight on for about 100 yards, then turn right along a wide gravel track and follow it to a crosstrack where the gravel curves left. Cross over and follow the path almost opposite for a few yards. Now the path divides.

❼ Keep on down the left hand of the two paths. This path is roughly parallel with the A35 which is on your right though not visible. You may like to make a short detour at this point. You will see a small wooden gate on your right leading to a fenced area.

This surrounds the recently restored Costicles Pond. I was told by Mr Green, a local keeper, that before the pond had been allowed to degenerate into an overgrown marsh, he remembered skating parties

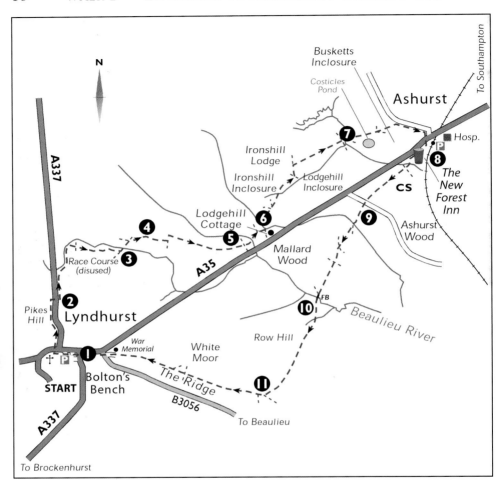

coming through the Forest from nearby Ashurst Lodge when the pond was frozen over. They would arrive with torches and hampers to skate by moonlight. It must have been a noisy lively scene. Now the pond has been restored it provides a home for rare wildlife.

Continue along the track heading east. Ignore the first green ride you pass on

your left but turn left down the next track which leads you to a gate opening into Woodlands Road. Turn right and follow the road as it curves right to meet the A35.

Just over the bridge on your left you will find shops and cafés and an excellent pub, the Happy Cheese. Nearby is another good place for a meal and a pint – overlooking the

Frederick Leigghton's beautiful fresco in Lyndhurst church depicting the parable of 'The Wise and Foolish Virgins'. Local Lyndhurst girls acted as models although some hesitated, not wishing to be known as foolish virgins.

Forest with a playground for the children – The New Forest Inn. This old inn was originally built as a hunting lodge and was visited by Queen Victoria.

❽ Cross the A35 at the top of Woodlands Road and turn right past the New Forest Inn. Turn left through the gate leading to Ashurst campsite but do not follow the road to the site. Instead, turn right and make your way over the grass and heath with the campsite beyond the trees on your left and the A35 about 200 yards away on your right. There is no clear track but just walk straight ahead parallel with the main road. Soon you will see a small wood on your right between you and the road. Walk along the edge of the wood with the trees on your right. This is a relic of an old wood

where some magnificent pollarded trees survive all with their trunks protected by holly and their branches draped with ivy and honeysuckle.

❾ Cross straight over a lane which leads to Ashurst Lodge and keep straight ahead past a Forestry Commission barrier with the A35 still about 200 yards away on your right. The path becomes clear winding through woods and over small heaths gradually bearing left further away from the road. Just after you cross a footbridge over a ditch the path divides. Ignore the path which bears slightly left and keep straight on over a more open area towards the outlying fringes of Mallard Wood. As you enter the wood the way becomes a wide green path.

Mallard Wood is one of the Forest's finest oak and beech woods, classified by the Forestry Commission as 'ancient and ornamental'. It is the home of many wild creatures including badgers and deer.

You leave the wood to come out on the heath again and now a wide view stretches ahead of you. Across Longwater Lawn you will see our destination, The Ridge, a high belt of heathland east of Lyndhurst.

❿ Our path leads to a bridge over the Beaulieu River, still only a stream bordered in summer with yellow-flowered bog asphodel and starred with the white flowers of water crowfoot. The stones mark the boundary of Lyndhurst and Colbury parishes. Keep ahead and soon the path becomes raised and embanked to lead across some boggy areas. Here the air is heavy with the pungent scent of bog myrtle, sometimes given the much more attractive name of gold withey.

The path climbs a little to run to the left of a small hill crowned with pines.

Beneath the pines the ground is dry and firm. This is a perfect place to pause and enjoy the peace and timeless quality of the Forest. Follow the path as it rises gently towards The Ridge. You will see Lyndhurst church spire on your right. When you gain the crest of The Ridge you meet a wide white track.

⓫ Turn right and follow the track in the direction of the church spire. The Ridge which you are now following is part of the boundary of Park Pale, an area defined as a deer park in 1291. Soon you will see the dome-shaped hill crowned with trees just east of Lyndhurst that features on the village sign. The mound possibly dates from the Iron Age and is called Bolton's Bench after Lord Bolton who was Lord Warden of the Forest in 1688. You pass a small chapel on your right and the cricket pitch on your left. Our way becomes a metalled road leading you past The Bench, to the left of the war memorial. When you meet the main road turn left to walk up Lyndhurst High Street and so back to the car park.

ACRES DOWN:
A RIDGE WALK

Length: 7¹/₂ miles, shorter walk 4 miles

Pilmore Gate Heath.

Starting point: Swan Green car park, just west of Lyndhurst. (GR 286 085) Turn off the A35 following the sign for Emery Down. After about 50 yards cross the cattle grid and turn left into the car park. **Public Transport:** Bus to Lyndhurst, walk west on the A35 for about ¹/₄ mile then turn right for Emery Down. Map: Ordnance Survey Outdoor Leisure 22. The point where the shorter walk leaves the longer route is given in the text in bold type. **Refreshments:** Cafés, pubs and restaurants in Lyndhurst. The New Forest Inn, Emery Down. The village shop for pies and savouries. Acres Down Farm for cream teas, open April and May on Sundays and Mondays, every day in June, July and August.

Ridge walks are rare in the Forest as it is generally low-lying, but when they do occur they give rare insights into the Forest's beauty with all its contrasting shades of woodland and far-reaching views. This ridge walk is my favourite. There is no difficulty in finding it – no trackless wastes to cross – but it will lead you to the real heart of the Forest.

The Walk

❶ From the car park entrance turn left and follow the road to the top of the hill overlooking the attractive hamlet of Emery Down. The scattered houses of the village are dotted along the hillside, their gardens making colourful oases among the dips and hollows. The road bears left past the church built in warm red brick in 1864 from designs by William Butterfield. The church was the gift of Admiral Boultbee. Further down the road you pass a group of almshouses overlooking a courtyard. These were also given to the village by the Admiral and are known locally as 'Boultbee's cottages'.

❷ Walk through the village to the road junction in front of the New Forest Inn and turn right following the road signed for Stoney Cross. Continue past a private drive on your left. As you follow

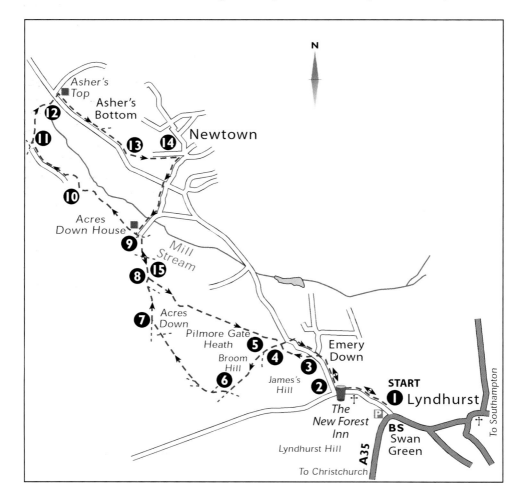

the road you may have to watch for traffic at busy times. After about ¼ mile, just past a lane on the right, you come to a turning on the left a few yards past a letter box.

❸ Turn left up the gravel track and when it divides continue along the right-hand track which leads past some houses on your right.

❹ When the gravel gives way to green Forest lawns, turn right along a white path leading over the grass to enter the oak and beech woods at the northern edge of James's Hill. After about 60 yards the path divides. Keep ahead along the grassy left hand path. Follow the path through the trees for about 80 yards to a more open area where a path joins our way from the right.

❺ We turn left along this path but it is not easy to see at first. It runs just to the left of a small gully. Turn left through the trees with the gully close on your right to descend to a wide green clearing. The path is clear now leading ahead over the grass towards the woods of Broom Hill Inclosure. Follow the path through the woods as it curves round the foot of James's Hill.

James's Hill is a rarity in the Forest: isolated, over 300 feet high and still retaining a thick gravel topping. In the past the gravel made it valuable. On an old map of 1789 it is called 'gravel hill' and former diggings remain on the top. Until recent times all main Forest roads were gravel. The road from Ashurst through Lyndhurst —now the A35 – was gravelled up to the beginning

of the Second World War! But the less important ways through the Forest were mere mud tracks. Coaches and carriages had to be preceded by armed postillions with a guide. At night large circular horn lanterns holding three candles each known as 'moons' were fixed to poles and attached to the stirrups of the postillions.

Continue for about ¼ mile, ignoring all side tracks, until you come to a crossing path. You need to navigate carefully here as the path is not well defined. (It is important never to turn left as you walk through this Inclosure!)

❻ Turn right and follow the path sloping a little downhill towards an open glade. Keep to the main path as it bears left past a joining path on the right. Now you can see our objective clearly, Acres Down, a high ridge of heath and gorse-covered moorland rising ahead just a little to your right. When the path divides at the edge of the glade keep ahead along the right-hand path to cross the glade and enter the woods. Continue over a small stream. The path rises towards an open area and forks. Take the right-hand path and now the high, smooth ridge of moorland is directly ahead. Our way is clear, over the heath in the valley, then winding to the top of the ridge through low gorse bushes and groves of silver birches. Climb to the top and pause to look back.

You are standing high on the heath of Acres Down. All around you spread billowing waves of woodlands. The dark pines of the Highland Water valley contrast with the bright greens of the oaks and beeches of

The attractive almshouses in Emery Down were built in 1864. They were the gift of Admiral Boultbee and are known locally as Boultbee's Cottages.

Broom Hill and Wood Crates, James's and Lyndhurst Hills. There is a glimpse of Southampton, framed by these massed woods, and far away on the horizon, the soft blue of the Isle of Wight hills. This is a place to rest the spirit!

Walk over the ridge along the main path ignoring all side tracks until a track joins your way on the left.

❼ Keep to the main track as it bears right to run along the crest of the ridge with beautiful views over the valley on your left. After about ¼ mile you pass a joining track on the right. Keep ahead as the path dips and continues through a wooded area. After a few yards you will see a grassy path on your right which

leads along the side of a valley, over Pilmore Gate Heath.

❽ At this point (GR 269 094), if you prefer the shorter walk, turn right to follow this path which crosses the heath and meets the minor road for Stoney Cross which we followed at the beginning of the walk. At the road turn right to return through Emery Down to Swan Green car park. If you would like tea before returning, make a short detour first. Do not turn right immediately but keep on past a Forestry Commission barrier to a crosstrack. Turn left down the lane following a sunken lane. The tea room at Acres Down Farm is opposite the foot of the lane.

To continue our longer walk keep

ahead past the Forestry Commission barrier to the crosstrack and bear left down the sunken lane to face Acres Down Farm.

9 Before the Farm, turn left along a lane. Pass a lane on your left which leads to a car park, and keep ahead to pass a sign on the right 'Acres Down House and Cottage only'. Follow the track, leaving the house and cottage on your right, and when the gravel ends keep straight on following the path up the heath ahead. A little to the left of our path a tall stand of pines shades an old marl pit.

You will find pits like this throughout the Forest. Forest land is generally poor but in some places better quality soil can be found. One of the commoners' rights was 'the right of marl' allowing them to fertilise their land by spreading over it good soil, leaving pits like this. Marling was a skilled craft with a host of technical terms, songs, customs and sayings attached to it. Two sayings I have heard are 'he that marls moss shall have no loss' and conversely 'he that marls clay flings all away'. Gangs of marlers went from farm to farm, one of whom was chosen as 'Lord of the Soil'. Passers-by were asked for money and at the end of the week there was a celebration at the local inn. When a whole area was finished, everyone joined in – marlers, farmworkers, neighbours and tenants – with drinks and a good supper for all.

Keep to the path as it winds over heathland dotted with trees and through small woods. The path rises to face a path leading left beside wooden rails.

10 Ignore this and bear a little right to continue heading north-east over a boggy patch. Keep ahead until you come to a wide green crosstrack. If you look left the track leads to a gate beside a trig point.

11 We turn right to follow the main track over the heath with trees close on the left. When the track divides follow the main track still as it bears right towards an oak and beech wood. Walk through the glades at the edge of the wood, shaded by some huge trees, the ground deep in mast.

We are heading towards the minor road from Emery Down to Stoney Cross again. Just before you come to the road, the path divides. Follow the left-hand path towards a house which is on the opposite side of the road.

12 Cross the road and turn right to walk along the heath with the road on your right. Continue beside the road past a bridleway sign pointing left. We do intend turning left but our way is about 100 yards further on.

13 Pass a letterbox and a drive signed 'Access to private properties only' and turn left past a Forestry Commission barrier. Bear left over the grass with bushes on your left to meet a wide track leading downhill into a valley of small fields. Follow the lane as it leads through the farming countryside surrounding Minstead village.

14 The track meets a lane in Newtown. Turn right for a few yards to a corner by

Broom Hill Inclosure.

a phone box then turn right again to walk uphill to rejoin the Stoney Cross road. Go straight over the road and walk down the lane ahead signed for Acres Down. Cross a stream, Bartley Water (there is a bridge on the left) then walk up the lane to pass Acres Down Farm. Retrace your steps up the sunken lane and when the lane levels and curves left turn right to pass the Forestry Commission barrier and retrace your earlier route as far as the first grassy path on the left. This is the path I mentioned earlier as a quick return route for the shorter walk.

⓯ Turn left to follow the path downhill through woods and over Pilmore Gate Heath. You pass a small pond covered in cream and scarlet waterlilies in June. The path becomes a wide gravelled track and brings you to the Stoney Cross road close to Emery Down. Turn right to walk through the village to return to Swan Green car park.

ASHURST

Ashurst is a pleasant leafy village on the north-eastern border of the New Forest, only seven miles from Southampton. It is well served by buses and trains. There are several restaurants and two excellent pubs. It tends to be overlooked by walkers but the village is the gateway to some of the most beautiful and historic parts of the Forest as you will discover on this walk. The scenery is exceptionally varied with open heaths, green Forest lawns cropped short by the ponies and some of the finest of the Forest's great oak and beech woods, termed 'ancient and ornamental' by the Forestry Commission.

The walk includes a stroll through one of the finest of these, Matley Wood. At quiet times you should see fallow deer with their wide spreading antlers and distinctive white rump and the smaller reddish-brown roe with their small upright antlers. Apart from their appearance the deer have their own way of organising their lives. Fallow deer gather in herds and in the rutting season, around October and November, the buck will stand guard over his harem of hinds, roaring defiance at all challengers. Roe prefer to live in small family groups and will often be seen with their fawns.

ASHURST AND MATLEY WOOD

Length: 6 miles

The bridge over the Beaulieu river on the way to Matley Wood.

Starting point: Ashurst car park, close to the entrance to Ashurst Hospital. (GR 334 103) Turn off the A35 in front of the row of shops in Ashurst. Drive past the shops on your left and the Happy Cheese pub and continue over the drive to the hospital to the car park on your left. **Public Transport:** Frequent bus service to Ashurst (shops) or take the train to Ashurst Station. From the station turn right over the railway bridge then right again to pass the shops to the car park. **Map:** Ordnance Survey Outdoor Leisure 22. **Refreshments:** Cafés and restaurants in Ashurst also two pubs, the Happy Cheese and the New Forest Inn. **Campsite:** Ashurst. To start the walk from the campsite, turn right from the camp site entrance, cross the railway bridge, then turn right again to pass the shops to the car park.

This walk from Ashurst, although only six miles round, takes you through pine woods and across open heaths to one of the oldest woods in the Forest, Matley Wood. On the way you can form your own conclusions about a Forest mystery that has occupied historians for centuries. We return through Ironshill Inclosure, a name with links to Roman times.

THE WALK

1 From the car park entrance turn left towards the railway line, then shortly after turn left again to go through the gate which leads you to the wide lawns beside the railway. Follow the path ahead with the edge of Churchplace Inclosure on your left and the railway on your right. Go through a gate.

2 Ignore the track leading right to a bridge over the line and the obvious gravel track ahead and turn immediately left along a green ride. (This may seem unlikely as the ride is not clear at first but it soon becomes a clear wide way.) The ride brings you to a gravel track. Bear left along the track for a few yards then follow it straight ahead to a crosstrack.

3 Follow the gravel track curving right as it climbs gently uphill to run to the right of a knoll crowned with oaks and beeches. This is Churchplace, one of several marked on New Forest maps.

These Churchplaces, like the death of William Rufus in the Forest, are still not fully explained. No love was lost between the Saxon chroniclers and William the Conqueror. When he declared this part of southern England his own exclusive hunting Forest they recorded, with appropriate venom, his destruction of the Saxon villages within its precincts. Even worse, because it was sacrilege, was his alleged destruction of churches. Accounts in the chronicles vary but between 20 and 40 churches are supposed to have been destroyed. Are the Churchplaces dotted about the Forest the sites of some of these Saxon churches? Certainly this knoll would have made an ideal site as it was a high vantage point at the junction of several tracks. The chroniclers are confused about the numbers and as William Cobbett observed as he rode through the Forest in 1823, it is hard to imagine that the poor soil of the Forest could ever have supported sufficient people to require so many churches. The mystery remains. I explored Churchplace and discovered some curious ridges and rounded embankments. Could they have been the foundations of a wooden Saxon church?

Continue along the gravel track into Deerleap Inclosure. William Gilpin, vicar of Boldre in the 18th century, explains how this inclosure got its name.

'Here a stag was once shot' he writes 'which in the agony of death, collected his force, gave a bound, which astonished those who saw it. It was immediately commemorated by two posts, which were fixed at the two extremities of the leap ... the space between them is somewhat more than eighteen yards.'

4 When you come to the next crosstrack turn right and follow the gravel track downhill towards the railway line. At the foot of the hill the gravel track begins to curve right. Leave the gravel and turn left through a gate leading to open heathland. Turn right to cross a bridge over the railway.

At the other side of the line the path leads over a stream – a very young Beaulieu river. A few yards after the stream, our path divides. Keep to the right-hand track. Our way now winds through open heath towards the trees of

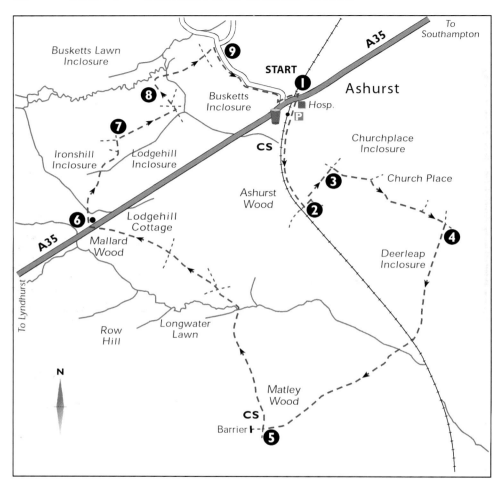

Matley Wood directly ahead. Walk through the outlying fringe of silver birches into the soft green glades of the wood shaded by ancient oak and beech trees.

All sorts of wildlife love Matley. It is the home of deer, badgers, foxes and squirrels of course, and the smallest and rarest of the woodpecker family the lesser spotted woodpecker. Every glade is rich with woodland flowers and ferns.

Follow the main path through Matley Wood until about 70 yards ahead you see a barrier.

❺ Do not continue to the barrier but take a path on the right leading downhill through the trees to the northern edge of

The keeper's cottage at the approach to Lodgehill Inclosure.

the wood. But at first the track is very faint. Look for a large whitened fallen tree carved with initials. Turn right past the tree and walk straight ahead downhill and the path soon becomes clear. When you come out of the trees you will see a well-defined path leading ahead through some gorse, then out over the open heath. The path crosses the moor to a bridge over Beaulieu River. Over the bridge another heath opens before you. Follow the path over the heath towards Mallard Wood. From the bridge our path bears very slightly left. About half-way over the heath go over a crosstrack. When the path divides, follow the left-hand path in the direction of the nearest trees. Keep straight on over another crosstrack to enter Mallard Wood. This

is another ancient wood with some particularly fine unpollarded beech trees. Cross a little heath to walk through the most northerly part of Mallard Wood. Go straight over all crosstracks and soon you will see the main A35 ahead. The path bears left to take you to a gate and stile beside the road.

On the other side of the A35, a little to your left, you will see Lodgehill Cottage.

❻ Cross the road and go through the gate to the left of the cottage into Lodgehill Inclosure. A few yards further on keep ahead along a gravel track. When you come to a crosstrack go straight across following the track immediately ahead with Ironshill Inclosure on your left.

In Matley Wood.

The name has an interesting story to tell, a story which takes us back 1,000 years before the Normans, perhaps even to pre-Roman times. East Hampshire was always rich in iron ore and in early days the ore was brought to the New Forest where there was a plentiful source of charcoal to be smelted. The name Ironshill occurs in other parts of the Forest also. High ground was essential to enable the wind to fan the tall cylindrical furnaces in which the iron ore was packed between layers of charcoal. From the coins and pottery which have been found in cinder heaps, these foundries were working in Roman times. Later, much more elaborate smelting works were built in the valleys using water power to drive huge hammers like the one at Sowley Pond, near Beaulieu, whose thudding became a characteristic sound of the New Forest.

Continue along the track until you see a wide grassy track on the left leading to gates and the private land around Ironshill Lodge.

❼ Turn right at this point to follow a track heading due east towards Ashurst. Follow the track as it bears round to the left, past two joining tracks on the right and the left.

❽ Take the next right along a gravel track, just before a stream with a footbridge. This brings you to a gate.

❾ Go through the gate and turn right to follow a minor road, Woodlands Road. The road bears right uphill to meet the A35 just before the railway bridge. Ashurst station is opposite. Turn right to return to the campsite or left over the bridge to return to your car.

BROCKENHURST

Brockenhurst means 'the badgers'wood'. Badgers are particular about where they live. They like old woods with great trees whose roots have worked the earth soft so they can excavate their setts easily and they insist on plentiful supplies of drinking water. Brockenhurst fulfils these conditions perfectly as it lies among glorious old woodlands and is interlaced with streams.

Like all Forest villages Brockenhurst spreads itself in a comfortable fashion over heaths and around green lawns cropped close by ponies. Wander down any of the little lanes that apparently lead nowhere and you will come across scenes that seem untouched by time: clusters of old cottages defended against the grazing ponies and donkeys by immensely thick hedges nearby, or one of Brockenhurst's many streams shaded by enormous trees which spread twisting coils of roots around its banks. And you will find, standing alone on a hill overlooking the Forest, a church older than the *Domesday Book*.

Brockenhurst is easily reached by bus and train and makes an ideal centre for a Forest holiday. There is accommodation to suit all pockets and a large campsite. The village has many fascinating places to explore particularly north of the village around the Balmer Lawn Hotel. The hotel served as a Marshalling Area Headquarters during preparations for the D-Day landings in 1944. The troops erected an inn sign, 'The Duck and Ducklings', showing a duck leading her family across the water. Near the hotel in Balmer Lawn Road you will find New Forest Wagons who offer leisurely wagon rides through the Inclosures.

Ponies using a bridge to cross the stream in Culverley Meadow.

BROCKENHURST VILLAGE RAMBLE

Length: 2 miles

Brockenhurst church dates back to Saxon times and is mentioned in the Domesday Book.

Starting point: Brockenhurst central car park off the main street, Brookley Road, opposite the Post Office. (GR 299 023) There is a four hour limit but that will give you plenty of time to complete this short ramble, visit some of Brockenhurst's interesting shops and perhaps enjoy a meal in one of the village's many excellent pubs, cafés and restaurants. **Public Transport:** Brockenhurst is well served by buses and trains. **Map:** Ordnance Survey Outdoor Leisure 22. **Campsite:** Hollands Wood, close to the north of the village beside the A337.

Everyone can enjoy this easy stroll around the village. Forest villages tend to tuck their treasures away and you must leave the main streets to find them. We also explore some of the surrounding countryside and discover one of Brockenhurst's hidden gems.

THE WALK

1 Return to the car park entrance at the junction with Brookley Road. On the corner you will see a brick plinth supporting a cast-iron tyre plate, recovered from the site of the village forge. It was used to hold the wooden wheels while the hot metal tyres were fitted.

2 Turn right down Brookley Road and cross the bridge beside the water-splash. Turn left along the minor road, pass a road on the left and you will see a fence on your left round the last house before a green Forest lawn.

3 Turn left over the grass. This is Culverley, the 'dove's meadow'. Continue ahead with trees on your left to cross two small bridges and follow the path past the school to the B3055.

4 Cross the road, turn left and walk beside the road for only a few yards to a footpath sign on the right. Turn right and follow a narrow path between gardens to cross a close. Directly ahead you will see a small wooden gate leading to a footbridge over the railway. Cross the bridge and go through the small gate ahead which leads you to a meadow path shaded by massive oaks. Keep straight ahead with a fence on your right. The path runs high along the side of hollows and embankments dense with thickets of wild roses. Cross a stile to the A337.

5 Turn left to walk beside the road for only about 50 yards – watch children and dogs here because of the traffic – to a lane on your right signed for St Nicholas' church. (You can shorten the distance beside the busy road by cutting the corner across a grassy area on your right.)

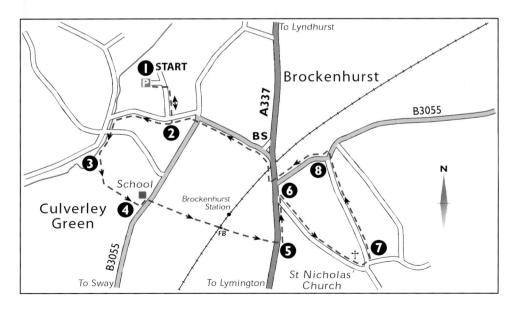

❻ Walk up the lane to the church. As the lane bears a little left to reveal the south front of the church you are faced with a building full of homely charm.

There has been a church here since Saxon times and Saxon herring-bone masonry is incorporated in the walls. Beside the south entrance a carved mass clock worked like a sundial to indicate the times for mass. The chevron mouldings over the doorway show Norman architecture at its best. There is more fine Norman carving inside. The curtained and cushioned 'Squire's Pew' must have concealed many of that gentleman's less attentive moments! On the wall beside the pew is a picture of Harry 'Brusher' Mills, a handsome bearded figure who has become part of Forest lore. He lived in a hut in the woods and caught snakes, much valued for their use in medicine. Walk down the hill through the churchyard. His grave is in the churchyard near the New Zealand war graves and Memorial on the east side of the central level. More than 100 New Zealand, Indian and other soldiers died in the base hospital at Brockenhurst during the First World War. The Imperial War Graves Commission ordered the replacement of the original wooden crosses with engraved headstones and erected the splendid memorial. Each year a service is held in their memory on the Sunday nearest to Anzac Day.

Apart from Sunday services, the church is open May to September from 2.30pm to 6pm every afternoon.

❼ Leave the lane which curves right and turn left down a track that tunnels beneath the trees downhill to the right of the churchyard. This brings you to a minor road – Mill Lane.

❽ Turn left to walk back to the A337 which you join almost opposite the station.

On the junction you pass Butts Cottages, named after the Butts, or targets once set up in every English village for archery practice in the days when every young villager was bound by law to grow accustomed to using the long bow. Only by practising from boyhood could they grow strong enough to bend the deadly yew bows that wrought such havoc at Agincourt and Crecy.

Turn right over the level crossing and bear left passing the island on your right to walk down Brookley Road. Keep straight on over the crossroads and you will see the car park entrance on your right.

BROCKENHURST AND THE BOLDRE RIVER: IN THE STEPS OF 'BRUSHER' MILLS AND W. H. HUDSON

Length: 6 miles

Roydon Manor. W. H. Hudson, author of Hampshire Days, *came to live here in 1902.*

Starting point: Brockenhurst Station (GR 301 020). **Public Transport:** Brockenhurst is well served by buses and trains. **Map:** Ordnance Survey Outdoor Leisure 22. **Refreshments:** Pubs, cafés and restaurants in the village. **Campsite:** Hollands Wood just north of the village beside the A337.

On this fascinating ramble you will see some of the Forest's most beautiful countryside as we walk through great woods of beech and oak and follow the bank of the Boldre river (sometimes called the Lymington river). We visit the oldest church in the Forest with its Memorial to the New Zealand and

Indian soldiers who gave their lives in the First World War. Close by is the grave of a Forest character, the adder-catcher 'Brusher' Mills. We cross the park surrounding what was in former times the powerful Brockenhurst Manor and enjoy a fine view of Roydon Manor, once the home of the naturalist W. H. Hudson who wrote about the Forest and its wildlife in *Hampshire Days*.

THE WALK

❶ From the station turn right in the direction of Lymington passing Mill Lane on your left. A little further on you come to a lane on your left signed for St Nicholas' church.

❷ Follow this quiet lane as it leads uphill between high hedges spiked with blackthorn and draped with trails of honeysuckle. The church is set back from the road on your left.

Like all old Forest churches, Brockenhurst church stands on top of a hill to serve as a landmark for travellers. The Saxons built a church here and you will find Saxon herringbone masonry incorporated in the lower part of the wall between the south doorway and the east end of the nave. The Domesday Book *records the existence of a church at 'Broceste' which is how the Norman scribes spelled the name of the village. The oldest part of the present building dates from the 12th century. Norman features include the arch over the south doorway decorated with chevron mouldings and the font with its lead-lined bowl of Purbeck stone. Don't miss the curtained 'Squire's Pew'. It is like a small room with seats all round.*

On the left of the south porch is an enormous yew tree. The creased and pleated trunk measures 15 feet round. It is also mentioned in the Domesday Book.

Walk down the hillside churchyard north of the church to see the memorial to the New Zealand and Indian soldiers who lie here. During the First World War Brockenhurst was the home of a base hospital. Close by is the grave of a Forest legend, 'Brusher' Mills. You will recognise his grave by the carving of 'Brusher' on the headstone.

He was called 'Brusher' because one of his occupations was to sweep the loose snow off the ice on Brockenhurst pond to clear the surface for skaters. He made his living, though, from the adders he caught in the Forest. He was what the Romanies call a sap engro – a snake catcher. C. J. Cornish, writing about the Forest in 1894, describes him as 'a strikingly handsome man'. The ointment made from adder fat, Cornish tells us, was good for 'sprains, black eyes, poisoning with brass, bites by rats and horses, rheumatic joints and sore feet in men and dogs'. 'Brusher' loved animals and cared for any sick ones he came across. As a sideline he would entertain travellers with the snakes he kept in his pocket. His headstone shows him twirling a handful of lively-looking snakes outside his Forest home, a simple wigwam of branches covered with turf. One evening he returned home to find his hut destroyed by vandals and it is said that this upset him so much he became ill. He died shortly afterwards. But the Forest will never forget him.

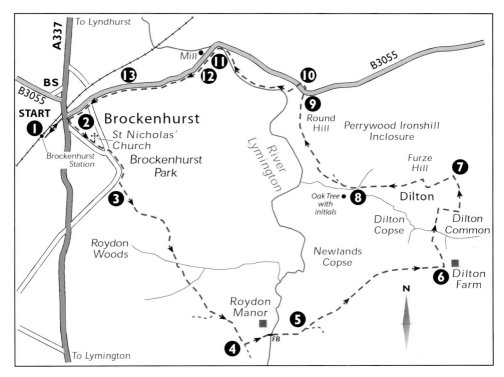

From the church, follow the road as it curves right to a bridleway on the left opposite a farm entrance.

3 Turn left along the path which runs along the southern boundary of Brockenhurst Park. This is part of the land belonging to Brockenhurst Manor whose history, like that of the church, can be traced back to the Domesday Book.

In Norman times, although the Forest was the property of the monarch, the lord of the manor could retain his land, graze his animals and gather fuel, in the words of Domesday 'quit and free from verderers and foresters without hindrance from the king'.

But conditions were attached. During the reign of Henry II, the Lord of the Manor, William Spilman, was required to entertain the king when he came hunting. His son was required to serve the king for eleven days in the event of war.

The old manor has been pulled down but a branch of the most recent holders of the Manor, the Morant family still lives in the area. In the WI publication, It Happened in Hampshire I read about a Dame's School established in Brockenhurst in 1812 by Lady Caroline Morant. Every year the children visited the Park for the school treat. At the head of the procession rode the headmistress, Miss Ash, in her donkey cart, the donkey dressed fore and aft in thick

The memorial to the New Zealand, Indian, and other soldiers who died in the base hospital at Brockenhurst during the First World War. The grave of 'Brusher' Mills is in the foreground.

white cotton trousers tied with blue and yellow ribbons, the Morant colours. In the schoolroom one of the former scholars recalls that the girls had their aprons pinned to Miss Ash's and the game was to fall over thus ripping off her apron. They evidently had a lively sense of mischief. One naughty boy, locked in a dark outhouse as a punishment discovered a store of apples in a corner and took just one bite out of each apple!

Follow the path to leave the parkland and go through a gate into Roydon Woods, a nature reserve rich in wildlife. Among the wealth of butterflies is one of the Forest's treasures, the Silver Washed Fritillary. Foxes and badgers are common, and the woods are home for five species of Forest deer – red, fallow, roe, muntjac and sika. Wild flowers include the blue-and-pink-flowered lungwort. The path leads down to a stream, over a bridge, then up through a gap in the old inclosure boundary to cross an open glade dotted with silver birches and willows. Cross another stream and continue uphill through a gate. A small plaque has been placed on the gate in memory of Colin Tubbs, a much-loved local ecologist. Continue ahead to a wide crossing track. Bear left for a short distance along this track and pass the lodge beside a private road to Roydon Manor on your left. Follow the footpath sign straight on until you come to a gate on the left leading to a path indicated with a bridleway sign.

Crossing the Boldre river, close to Roydon Manor.

❹ Turn left through gates and follow the path which soon reveals a splendid view of the 17th-century manor.

W. H. Hudson came to live here in 1902. He notes the date of the house, 1692, cut in a stone tablet in one of the rooms. Today the house has been restored from the rather ramshackle state he describes in his book Hampshire Days. 'Never have I known any human habitation' he writes, 'in a land where people are discovered dwelling in so many secret, green, out of the world places, which has so much of nature in and about it …a small old picturesque red-brick house with high pitched roof and tall chimneys, a great part of it overrun with ivy and creepers'. Passionately interested in wildlife, small insects fascinated him. Observing that female grasshoppers were often ignored by the males and often sat patiently alone for hours, he carried one into the house on a wild rose branch. There she remained for 16 days and when she had eaten all the berries on her branch he kept her alive with a varied diet which included bread-and-butter pudding and ginger beer!

Continue past the manor to cross the Boldre river by a wooden footbridge. The water appears exactly as Hudson describes it, 'the colour of old sherry'. Climb the path ahead through the wood and walk along the edge of Newlands Copse.

❺ At the top of a rise, when the path divides, keep straight on (left fork). Go through the gate at the end of the wood and follow the track straight ahead which runs over open farmland towards Dilton Farm.

❻ Just before the first farm building turn left along a wide fenced bridleway which bears half right to lead downhill and over a stream. Keep to the path as it climbs to run along the edge of Dilton Copse then turns right beside another wood. Our way then turns left again and climbs with the wood on the left and bushes on the right. On your left you pass some huts, the remains of a military encampment built here during the last war. When you come to a bridleway sign turn left and follow the concrete track through a gate.

❼ Turn left along another concrete track. When the concrete ends continue straight ahead down a gravel track to leave the bleakness of the heath behind and walk along a green valley with the scattering of houses that comprise Dilton on your left.

Cross a stream and keeping the stream on your left follow the path ahead to walk through Perrywood Ironshill Inclosure, a beautiful oak and beech wood. Always keeping the stream on your left, continue through the wood until you come to a glade dominated by a magnificent oak tree carved with initials.

❽ Turn right passing the tree on your left and take the left hand of the two tracks you will see ahead. Shortly you will see the fenced inclosure boundary parallel with your path on your left. Continue through the wood until the

trees thin and you leave the inclosure to cross a green lawn and pass a Forestry Commission barrier to the B3055.

❾ Turn left beside the road for just a few yards to a path leading left into Ivy Wood past three short wooden posts.

❿ Follow the path downhill through the trees over small wooden bridges to the bank of the Boldre river, then turn right with the river on your left and follow any of the paths close to the river bank. This is an enchanting riverside walk. You leave the wood and come to a road junction and a bridge with white railings on your left.

⓫ Turn left over the bridge along the minor road, Mill Lane.

Continue along the lane past the former mill for only about 150 yards to a gravel track on your left where you will see a footpath sign on a tree on your right.

⓬ Go through the small wooden gate to the right of the gravel track and follow the footpath sign along the northern edge of Brockenhurst Park. Mill Lane runs parallel with your route beyond a fence on your right. Keeping the fence close on your right continue over the parkland to go through another small gate to rejoin Mill Lane by the lodge at the northern entrance to the park. Opposite the lodge is a cottage with a large 'M' for Morant above the door.

⓭ Turn left to follow Mill Lane to the A337 and cross the road to return to Brockenhurst station.

BURLEY

Burley, in the south-west of the Forest, is very much a walkers' village. It has grown, as Forest villages do, in a relaxed way around its old manor and park forming several small communities. So just when you think you have found and finished with the village you go round a curve in the road, through a wood, or over the crest of a heath and there is another little green surrounded by houses and more gates into thickly-hedged gardens. The village is surrounded by glorious heaths and woods. West of the village a high ridge of moorland gives wonderful views over the Avon valley.

The view over Cranes Moor, where in the 6th century, Saxon fought Celt.

DRAGONS, SMUGGLERS AND BATTLES LONG AGO

Length: 6 miles

Burley Manor, now an hotel.

Starting point: Burley village car park. (GR 212 031) The public car park adjoins the car park for patrons of the Queen's Head pub at the junction of four roads at the head of Burley High Street. If the car park is full, drive up the road immediately opposite the pub to large car parks either side of the road. **Public Transport:** Buses stop at the Queen's Head. **Map:** Ordnance Survey Outdoor Leisure 22. **Refreshments:** The Queen's Head and excellent cafés and restaurants in the village.

The name Burley means 'a fortified place in a clearing' and in the past it was the scene of many conflicts. The embankments of an Iron Age hill fort crown the ridge west of the village and below the fort a Saxon warpath runs west to Ringwood in the Avon valley.

The village was a favourite haunt for smugglers bringing luxury goods from France during the 18th and early 19th centuries and their track still crosses Burley moor. And close by, on Beacon Hill, surely the most amazing fight of all took place when brave Sir Moris tackled the local dragon! Follow this walk and take a step back into Burley's fascinating past.

THE WALK

❶ Return to the car park entrance and turn left along a minor road, Chapel Lane, to a track on the right leading uphill signposted 'To the Church'.

❷ Turn right to walk up to the Victorian church of St John the Baptist. Consecrated in 1839 by Charles Sumner, Bishop of Winchester, this simple little church is particularly light and welcoming. The windows and memorial tablets tell their stories of Burley people. A stained-glass window is dedicated to the memory of Constance Applebee who pioneered women's hockey in America. She died in 1981 in her 108th year. On her 100th birthday she received a telegram from the American President as well as the customary telegram from the Queen.

From the church gate you have a fine view of Burley Manor in the valley surrounded by parkland.

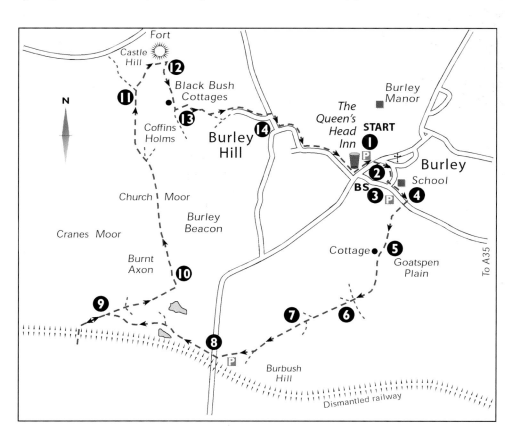

Although not mentioned in the Domesday Book *it is likely a manor stood here in Saxon times as no further grants of land would have been made after William the Conqueror enclosed the Forest in 1079. In 1550 a Tudor house was built on the site owned by the Batten family. This was replaced by a Georgian manor which was destroyed by fire in 1850. After the fire Colonel Esdaile had the central part of the house rebuilt in Tudor style. During the Second World War the manor was requisitioned by the Army. The lake was drained and many fine trees were cut down. One remains – a cedar, possibly about 150-years old – on the south lawn. The manor is now a hotel.*

Cross the road in front of the church and follow the path ahead past the vicarage on your right, through the trees. The path leaves the wood to keep straight on past the school to a minor road.

3 Turn left and follow the road for about 100 yards to a car park sign pointing right.

4 Turn right over the road and follow the gravel track past the car park sign. Beyond a Forestry Commission barrier you will see our path – a white track leading south over the heath. Follow this straight ahead over all crosstracks. This heath, Goatspen Plain, has a character all its own. The path dips and rises over shallow valleys and miniature hills presenting unexpected glimpses of a hidden Forest lawn, a half-concealed stream or a lonely wood.

Soon you come to a deeper valley with a white cottage and a barn to the right of your path.

5 Turn left in front of the cottage and follow the track past a Forestry Commission barrier along the valley and keep to the track as it bears right uphill to lead over the heath again. Across the heath on your right you will see the line of the old oak woods south of Burley. Follow the main track over all crosstracks until you come to a point where four tracks meet. There are two tracks directly ahead of you.

6 Take the left-hand of the two tracks and follow it downhill. A path branches right from our path and immediately our path forks.

7 Bear right at the fork in the direction of the minor road that runs from Burley due south to Thorney Hill. We aim to join the road at Burbush Hill car park just before the point where the road crosses a bridge over the disused railway. So keep to the track through a small belt of trees, over a green, to walk past Burbush Hill car park, leaving it on your left, to the road. The railway bridge is on your left.

8 Keeping the cutting through which the old railway runs on your left, cross the road and follow the path immediately ahead, running west, almost parallel with the railway.

You pass to the right of a small Forest pool where the path divides. Keep straight on (left-hand path). This attractive path over the heath leads you

A milestone at Burley commemorates the Treaty of Amiens: a brief halt in the Napoleonic Wars.

where three tracks meet. Keep walking directly ahead following the centre path uphill. Follow this path with Burley ridge still directly ahead. As you come close to the ridge you will see a pond over the heath on your right and meet a crossing track.

❿ Turn left to head north across Cranes Moor. The long ridge formed by Burley Beacon, Burley Hill and Castle Hill now rises on your right.

Cranes Moor feels like an old battlefield and as John Wise, the 19th-century Forest historian tells us, place names seem to prove it. We find 'Greater' and 'Lesser Castle Fields' and 'Barrows' (burial mounds) and 'Coffins'. There is a curious wood of twisted oaks and thorns marked significantly on the map as 'Burnt Axon'. No doubt they were battle axes! Over to the right Burley Beacon, where fires were lit in times of danger, frowns down on us and here, evidently, be dragons! A document of uncertain date in Berkeley Castle tells the story of a fight between a certain Sir Moris Barkley and a 'devouring dragon'. The document reads: 'Sir Moris Barkley the son of Sir John Barkley, of Beverston, being a man of great strength and courage, in his time there was bred in Hampshire near Bisterne a devouring dragon, who doing much mischief upon men and cattel and could not be destroyed but spoiled many in attempting it, making his den near unto a beacon. This Sir Moris Barkley armed himself and encountered with it and at length overcame and killed it but died himself soon after'. There are two Dragon Fields at Bisterne and the pub at Brook is called the Green Dragon. The redoubtable Sir Moris was also Lord of

downhill through a small glade, then up into a pine wood. Walk through the wood and downhill again where a path joins our way from the right. We shall be retracing our steps later to follow this path but the wood ahead is so lovely I would like you to see it first! So continue along the path through some very tall Scots pines to another bridge over the railway. Pause here among these silent pine groves to absorb their scent and colour.

❾ Retrace your steps with Burley ridge now directly ahead and bear left at the first fork. Shortly you come to a point

The view over Cranes Moor, where in the 6th century Saxons fought Celt.

the Manor of Minstead and Brook. *Thanks to Sir Moris we may go on our way in safety!*

Follow the track over Cranes Moor, past the foot of Burley Hill. This is one of several tracks used by smugglers in the past, leading from Thorney Hill, over Cranes Moor then north to Picket Post beside the present A31 where there is said to be a bricked-up cellar in which were stored contraband goods. Keep straight on over all crosstracks. The path dips into a gully then climbs again. Continue along the path a little further until at the foot of Castle Hill the path makes a conspicuous fork.

⓫ Ignore the path leading ahead to a minor road and turn right to climb the hill aiming for the corner of an oak wood at the top of Castle Hill. As you climb higher you cross ditches and embankments and if you look back you will see two loaf-shaped hillocks guarding the approaches to this ancient hill fort.

A castle, in the Forest, means an Iron Age or pre-Roman fort or protected settlement. Today the encircling ditches and embankments remain, often enclosing a large area where the first settlement could be made and in times of danger the whole village could gather with their animals for safety. Originally the embankments would have been crowned by high timber palisades with strong gates. The Forest forts date back to about 500 BC. Historians can tell us little about the part played by them during the early days of the Roman invasion in AD 43 but the Forest lay directly in the path of the Roman legion under Vespasian as he advanced to attack the great hill forts in Dorset. Later the area seems to have settled down peacefully under Roman rule. Pottery was made locally and at Sloden near Dockens Water some of which was exported to different parts of the empire.

Pause to enjoy the view from the hill fort. Below you, rolling heaths spread in waves to lead your eye over the Avon valley. A little to your right a break in the outline of the heath gives a glimpse of the Wiltshire Downs and to the left on a clear day you can see the tower of Christchurch Priory. Below Castle Hill the minor road running west from Burley through Crow to Ringwood has been identified as a Saxon warpath by John Wise and Heywood Sumner, both noted Forest historians. According to the newspaper of the time, The Anglo-Saxon Chronicle, *the New Forest was the scene of a major invasion by Saxon tribes under their leaders Cerdic and Cynric in* AD 495. *They landed at 'Cerdices ora', possibly Totton or Calshot, and advanced through the Forest to defeat the British at 'Natanleay', today's Netley Marsh. The name commemorates the loser, the British leader Natan-leod. The area took some time to subdue for it was not until* AD 519 *that the Saxons inflicted a conclusive defeat on the Britons close to the Avon at 'Cerdices ford', today's Charford, not far from Burley.*

⓬ Our return route starts by following the path south along the top of the ridge. So turn right to leave the hill fort on your right and follow this path.

⓭ Just past Black Bush Cottage turn left to cross a stile by a footpath sign and follow the woodland path as it winds downhill. Finally the path runs to the left of the private drive to Burley Hill House. Go through the iron gate to meet the road which leads from Burley to the A31.

⓮ Turn right to walk a few yards along the pavement then cross the road following the footpath sign and continue along a pleasant path with the road on your right bringing you to the foot of Burley High Street.

On the right you pass a milestone dated 1802. This seems to have been a busy year for milestone makers as there is another one erected in Burley in the same year on the left of the road opposite the Queen's Head. It has the words 'Rest and be Thankful' carved on one side and 'Peace returned 27 March 1802' on the other. This touchingly records the brief pause in the long Napoleonic wars which followed the Treaty of Amiens.

Walk up the High Street lined with many fascinating shops – perhaps reward yourself with a cream tea! – and turn left by the Queen's Head to return to your car or bus.

BURLEY VILLAGE AND HILL FORT

Length: 5 miles, shorter walk 3 miles

Burley Street, one of the small settlements around Burley village.

Starting point: Burley village car park. (GR 212 081) The public car park adjoins the car park for patrons of the Queen's Head pub at the junction of four roads at the head of Burley High Street. If the car park is full, drive up the road immediately opposite the pub to large car parks either side of the road. **Public Transport:** Buses stop at the Queen's Head. **Map:** Ordnance Survey Outdoor Leisure 22. **Refreshments:** The Queen's Head and excellent cafés and restaurants in the village.

There are several attractive routes from Burley to the ridge west of the village crowned by the embankments of an Iron Age hill fort. This walk approaches the fort from the east to enjoy splendid views over the Avon valley before taking you for a ramble round some of Burley's intriguing byways.

THE WALK

❶ Turn right from the car park entrance, passing the Queen's Head pub on your right, to the top of Burley High Street. Turn right to walk down through the village. Continue beside the road as far as Clough Lane.

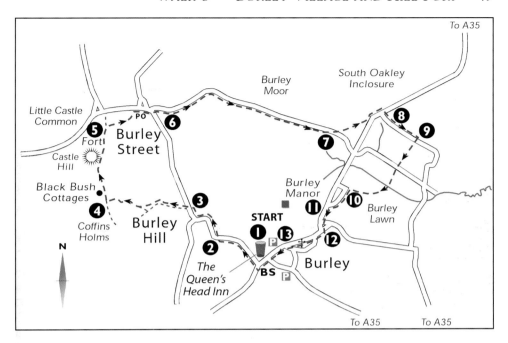

2 Opposite the lane, on the right, you will see a small gate and a raised footpath signed for Burley Street. Follow this attractive path with the road below you on the left and meadows on your right until it descends to the road. Continue along the pavement on the other side of the road for just a few yards to the gates of Burley Hill House. A public right of way leads through the right-hand gate (you will see an inconspicuous footpath sign pointing towards it).

3 Turn left through the gate and follow the fenced path which leads to the right of the drive to Burley Hill House then climbs uphill through a private wood. Keep to the fenced path through the trees, ignoring small gates on the right, to

cross a stile leading to a gravel track. You have now climbed the ridge sheltering Burley, but at this point trees mask your view of the valley.

4 Turn right past Black Bush cottages and follow the gravel track as it climbs a little more through woods to an open grassy area on the right encircled by the steep embankments of the Iron Age hill fort. Leave the gravel to walk round the fort and enjoy the view far over Cranes Moor and the Avon Valley to the soft blue haze of the Wiltshire Downs.

The Forest hill forts are small compared with those in neighbouring Dorset but in times of danger this would probably have provided a haven for a whole village and their animals.

Burley village.

Raised by the people of the Iron Age, around 500 BC, the fort was possibly the original Burley as the name means 'a fortified place in a clearing'. Below the fort you will see two small loaf-shaped hills which would guard the approach from the valley. The whole area must have been the scene of conflicts. On the map you will find 'Burnt Axon' and 'Coffin Holms'.

Return to the gravel track and turn left to continue our walk (the hill fort is on your left.) Ignore the first gravel track you pass on your right signed for Hilltop House and continue a little downhill to the next gravel track on your right.

5 Turn right and follow this track downhill past a riding stable to cross the grass and meet the road in Burley Street.

Turn right to the former village shop and post office. Although the shop and post office are now closed the original sign is still above the door. **If you wish you could take the shorter option and catch the bus to Burley from here. You will be back at the Queen's Head in just a few minutes.**

6 To continue the longer walk turn left opposite the former shop along Forest Road. The road leads over a ford (there is a bridge for walkers) and then bears right to cross Burley Moor. The road soon becomes a true Forest way with moorland on the left and a single row of houses overlooking the moor on the right. Walk over the heath, following the line of the road for about a mile. The road begins to curve sharply right.

❼ Before the curve, turn left over the grass leaving a house on your right. (It is the first house you see on the left of the road.) Keep straight ahead along the southern edge of South Oakley Inclosure to go through a gated area and cross to a minor road.

❽ Turn left beside the road for a few yards to Mill Lane on your right signed to Mill Lawn. Turn right to follow Mill Lane for about ¼ mile. Now look carefully for a five-bar wooden gate on your right. There is a footpath sign but as it is half-buried in a hedge and points away from the road down the path we are to follow it is not easy to see. Look for a small green notice advising dog owners to keep their pets on leads.

❾ Turn right through the gate and follow the narrow path which at first runs between gardens. Continue beside a paddock, climb a stile, and cross a footbridge over a stream. The path follows the side of a meadow, passing a wood on the right, to a stile. Cross the stile and a footbridge to follow a path through a belt of trees. A little to your right you will see a gravel track. Cross to the gravel and keep ahead, with grassy lawns and a pond overgrown with the brown tufts of reed mace on your left, towards a row of houses. Beyond the houses you will see a road leading to Burley but we will not join it yet!

❿ Turn left along the gravel in front of the houses, keeping them on your right. Continue past a Forestry Commission barrier for about 100 yards then turn right to the road.

⓫ Turn left beside the road. After about 60 yards the road curves right. Follow the road round the corner to a gravel track leading uphill on the left.

⓬ Turn left to follow this through woods to a T-junction. Turn right to the little Victorian church of St John the Baptist, beautifully situated on the wooded hillside.

This simple church is particularly light and welcoming. The windows and memorial tablets tell their stories of Burley people. One inscription reads: 'Emma Harding, 1873–1976, a faithful member of this congregation who continued to walk to church when past her hundreth year'. A stained-glass window is dedicated to another long-lived lady, Constance Applebee, who died in her 108th year. She pioneered women's hockey in America.

With the church on your right, walk down to the road.

⓭ Turn left to walk the few yards back to the Queen's Head and the car park.

THE HEART OF THE FOREST

A short walk almost anywhere in the Forest can reveal an astonishing variety of scenery. Gravel plateaux, sandy plains, rich clay soils and marshes all make their distinctive contribution to this diversity. In the central area, clay soils predominate and so it is here that we find most of the old woods of beech and oak – the 'ancient and ornamental' woodlands as the Forestry Commission call them – which are the pride of the Forest.

Here are the great pollards. These trees have had their tops cut off some time before 1698 when the practice was declared illegal so now they sprout several thick trunks spreading huge elbows over the Forest floor. A pollarded tree can live for over 800 years! Oak woods with their open glades are the favourite haunt of fallow deer with their Bambi-like fawns. You may also see our only native deer, the dainty red-brown roe. Insects abound in oak woods so birds flourish. Among many fascinating species, you will find the green and greater spotted woodpeckers and – in one of its last refuges – the much smaller lesser spotted or barred woodpecker. And hidden in the bracken you may come across one of the rarest of all Forest flowers, the wild gladiolus.

HOLIDAYS HILL AND THE KNIGHTWOOD OAK

Length: 5 miles

The Knightwood Oak, said to be the oldest oak in the Forest.

Starting point: Millyford car park, just east of Lyndhurst. Leave Lyndhurst along the A35 in the direction of Bournemouth. Turn right for Emery Down at Swan Green. Drive through Emery Down and immediately past the New Forest Inn turn left along the road signed for Bolderwood and Linwood. After about 1½ miles cross Millyford Bridge and the car park is on your right. (GR 268 079) **Public Transport:** Take the bus along the A35 in the direction of Bournemouth and alight at the stop on Burley Road Corner (GR 262 058). Facing the A35, turn left (away from Lyndhurst) and walk for about ½ mile to join the route of the walk at the approach to the southern branch of the Rhinefield Ornamental Drive. Your joining point is indicated in the text in bold type. **Map:** Ordnance Survey Outdoor Leisure 22. **Refreshments:** The New Forest Inn, Emery Down, or the village shop for pies and savouries.

This ramble through the woods around Lyndhurst takes you to one of the oldest and best-known trees in the New Forest, the Knightwood Oak. The route also includes an enchanting stroll through the glades of Brinken Wood and an attractive path beside the Highland Water stream. And, if you wish, you can discover more about the wildlife of the Forest as we return past the New Forest Reptile Centre. The Centre is open from 10am to 4.30pm, April to September.

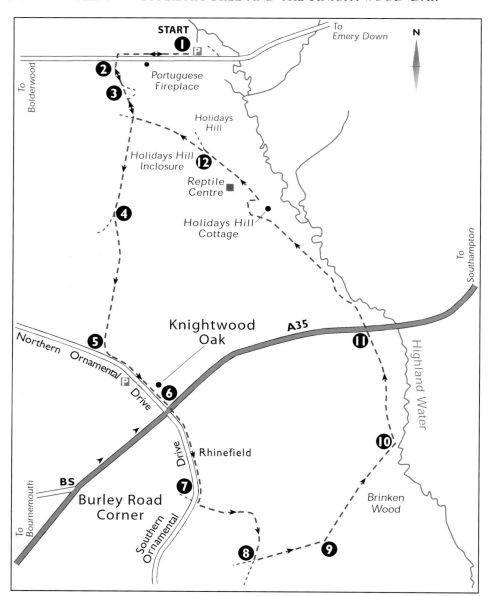

THE WALK

1 Walk back to the road from the car park. Turn right beside the road. On your left you pass an interesting reminder of the First World War, the Portuguese fireplace. During the war,

Portuguese soldiers came over to help the local forestry workers and built a camp here. The fireplace from their cookhouse has been restored as a memorial to them.

② About 100 yards past the fireplace you will see a gate on the left and a gravelled track. Turn left through the gate to enter Holidays Hill Inclosure.

Holidays Hill was one of the first Inclosures to be made in the Forest in 1676. It was made by order of Charles II who was concerned about his stock of timber. In 1670 he had appointed a Royal Commission to investigate the state of the Forest, which, partly as a result of the Civil War, had been neglected. As a result 300 acres were enclosed as a nursery for young oaks. We can still trace some survivors in woods like Holidays Hill though many have been lost in storms.

③ Follow the gravel track until you come to a large grassy triangle. Take the track bearing right – our direction is south. Carry straight on over a crosspath to go through a gate. Continue for about 150 yards when the gravel track begins to curve right.

④ Leave the gravel and take the green path almost directly ahead. This runs downhill to cross a tiny stream then rises to lead through a mixed wood of oak, beech and pine. The path leads to a minor road, the Bolderwood Ornamental Drive.

⑤ Turn left and a few yards along the drive, gravel paths on your left lead you to the Knightwood Oak.

The tree is certainly very old – some folk even say it was planted by William the Conqueror! It may not be able to claim as many centuries as that but carbon-dating proves it has been growing in this glade for over 500 years. At some time in its history the tree was pollarded which probably contributed to its long life. However, the practice does link the tree with William the Conqueror as pollard is derived from 'poil' the Norman-French word for a head.

Looking at this majestic tree it is easy to see why our even more distant ancestors regarded the oak as the king of trees and worshipped their gods beneath its branches. The oak must still be regarded as the monarch of the Forest. No other tree fosters as great a variety of wildlife. The rare Purple Emperor butterfly still finds a home on the tops of certain trees known as 'master oaks'.

The Knightwood Oak stands at the centre of the suitably-named 'Monarchs' Grove'. To mark the ninth centenary of the Forest in 1979, HM The Queen planted an oak close by. Eighteen oak trees were planted around the Knightwood Oak to represent all the recorded visits of reigning monarchs to the New Forest from William the Conqueror who declared the area a Royal Forest in 1079 to Edward VII in 1903.

Return to the Ornamental Drive and turn left to follow it to the A35. **Join the walk here if you started from the Burley Road bus stop.**

⑥ Cross the road to continue along the southern branch of the Ornamental Drive, now the Rhinefield Ornamental Drive. The road crosses a stream.

Portuguese workers helped local forestry workers during the First World War and had a hutted camp near Holidays Hill. The fireplace from their cookhouse has been restored as a memorial to them.

7 Take the next track on your left leading past a Forestry Commission barrier. Follow the track round a sharp bend to the right to a crosspath.

8 Turn left and follow the ride through a gate to the outskirts of Brinken Wood. A path leads you on through a strange landscape of hummocky green lawns, oaks twisted and bent into a host of angular shapes, and groves of elegant silver birches. Keep straight on crossing a bridge over a stream.

9 Now follow the grassy path bearing half-left through the birches. Walk through the fringe of birch trees and follow the path through the oak and beech trees of Brinken Wood.

The path leads you to a bridge over Highland Water.

10 Do not cross the bridge but turn left to follow a broad green path with the stream about 30 yards away on your right. Climb the stile beside the gate to the A35.

11 Cross straight over and walk up the gravel track ahead towards the Reptile Centre. As you approach the Centre you will see Holidays Hill Cottage, situated behind green Forest lawns. This is one of several lodges built for Forest keepers early in the 19th century. Each lodge had to have a garden and a paddock for a cow and a riding pony. Walk past the cottage then turn right through the gate to the reptile pens which are on your right.

The best time to see the snakes is a really warm summer's day. All our native reptiles are represented including the harmless olive-green grass snake, the rare smooth snake and our only poisonous reptile, the adder or viper, distinguished by zig-zag markings down its back. Adders are common in the Forest but there is no need to fear them as they are quick to get out of our way. This story about a very greedy Forest snake comes from the WI publication It Happened in Hampshire. *Apparently a girl with a bowl of porridge for breakfast allowed a snake to share it, dividing their portions equally. The snake gobbled its porridge and began to eat hers. Pushing it away she exclaimed 'eat your own side, speckleback!' This has become a local expression applied to anyone who wants more than his share.*

With the pens on your right walk straight ahead up the gravel track past a marker post representing a reptile. (This indicates the start of a short circular walk from the centre. There are six marker posts, each one showing a different native reptile.) After about 50 yards, at the top of the hill, look for a small green path leading left through the pine trees.

⓬ Turn left along this enchanting path – just one of the Forest's magical ways. This dips over a bridge and climbs to the gravel track we followed early in our walk. Turn right to retrace your steps along the track. **If you started from the Burley Road bus stop, turn left to continue the route of the walk.** Continue past the large grassy triangle leaving it on your right and follow the track to leave Holidays Hill Inclosure. Turn right to return to Millyford car park.

MINSTEAD AND FURZEY GARDENS

Length: 2 miles, but allow extra time to walk round Furzey Gardens

A 400-year-old cottage in Furzey Gardens.

Starting point: Parking area near the Trusty Servant inn, Minstead village. (GR 282 100) Minstead lies just to the north of Lyndhurst around a network of minor roads between the A31 and the A35. From Lyndhurst take the Romsey Road, the A337, and turn left following the signs for Minstead after about 1½ miles. There is parking in the village opposite the village green facing the Trusty Servant inn. If there is no room turn left in front of the inn up the lane to the church to park in front of the churchyard. **Public Transport:** Buses stop close to the village green. **Map:** Ordnance Survey Outdoor Leisure 22. **Refreshments:** The Trusty Servant inn. The village shop for snacks. Furzey Gardens has a tea room. The Honeysuckle Restaurant.

New Forest gardens, with their massed rhododendrons and azaleas which grow so well on the Forest's clay soils, are at their most beautiful in spring. This walk takes you to one of the loveliest, Furzey Gardens, where you will also be able to explore a 400-year-old cottage and visit a gallery stocked with New Forest crafts. We start from Minstead, a Forest village which is mentioned in the *Domesday Book* as 'Mintestede' – the place where mint grows.

THE WALK

❶ Before you start the walk have a look at the Trusty Servant inn sign. This depicts 'the trusty servant', a pig with padlocked snout so that he cannot disclose his master's secrets and stag's feet so that he can run errands quickly. It is copied from a picture in Winchester College whose motto 'manners makyth man' appears in the corner.

❷ Leave the Trusty Servant inn on your right and follow the little road which leads uphill signposted 'To the Church'. Overlooking the green on your left is the village war memorial and close by is an old well with a wooden cover. The stocks also stand on the green. On your right you pass an interesting building. This was built in 1897 as Minstead Technical School on a site presented by H. F. Compton of Minstead Manor to commemorate the 60th year of Queen Victoria's reign. At the top of the hill stands Minstead church.

It is built of traditional Forest materials, wattle filled with rubble and daub. Stone could only be spared for the arches and corners of the main walls. Originally it was thatched and some of the thin rafters that supported the thatch have been found above the present barrel roof. The archway over the north porch was carved early in the 13th century and is flanked by two heads, one most delicately carved and the other a much rougher version. Perhaps they are the work of a master and his apprentice. Inside the church is a very rare triple-decker pulpit. The sermon was preached from the top level, the Scriptures were read from the second. The lowest level was reserved for the parish clerk who had only 'Amen' to say at appropriate moments. The important family of Castle Malwood House, a mile or so away, had their own private seating arrangements – a cosy sitting room with a fireplace and its own entrance from an outside staircase.

Sir Arthur Conan Doyle lived in the parish at Bignell Wood and you will find his grave at the south end of the churchyard marked with a cross. He features Minstead in his stirring adventure story The White Company.

❸ Follow the path leading from the road to the right of the churchyard, leaving the church on your left. Go through a gate and continue with a hedge on your right. The path leads slightly downhill towards Manor Wood. Go through the gate to walk through this attractive wood of coppiced hazel, oaks and beech. Leave the wood through a gate and turn right to a road. Across the road, a little to your left, just before a crossing over a stream, you will see a sign pointing up a lane to the right signposted for Furzey Gardens. This is our way, but before turning right up the lane you might like to pause for a moment on the footbridge. The stream cuts its way through green lawns shaded by fine oak trees.

❹ Follow the lane uphill and keep straight on past a turning on the left to the next lane on the left signposted for Furzey Gardens. Turn left for the Gardens and after about 50 yards turn left through the entrance to the parking area. (If you wish to come by car drive

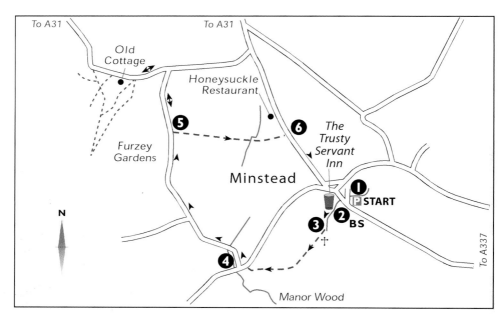

past the Trusty Servant in Minstead towards the A31 and take the first turning on the left which will lead you straight to Furzey.)

By the gate into the Gardens you will find a good map. Whenever you visit there is always colour and interest with many unusual plants and trees. To ensure that the more exotic plants would flourish, extra soil was brought here by horse and cart. One very rare azalea is said to have come from the garden of the Emperor of Japan. The Calico bush or Kalmia Latifolia grows well here, its clusters of pink, star-shaped flowers have a particularly clean and fresh look, exactly like well-starched calico. In spring the grass is bright with cyclaminus daffodils and purple crocuses. The charm of Furzey is that there are no sharp divisions between garden and forest. It merges almost

imperceptibly into the meadows and woods which surround it.

You can find out how New Forest workers once lived by exploring a 400-year-old cottage in the Garden. The kitchen with its enormous fireplace is unchanged. If you look up the chimney you will see the rail where the cottagers hung their bacon to be smoked. In the hearth is an assortment of 16th- and 17th-century kitchen utensils. To one side is a large circular bread oven and behind the oven part of the original wattle and daub cottage walls can be seen, built on a low brick foundation. New Forest cottagers built their homes out of whatever they could find and the roof beams and upstairs flooring are ships' timbers from the Tudor shipyards at Lymington. Upstairs there are only two very small bedrooms and yet a family of fourteen children once lived

Minstead church.

here! The children slept on straw on the floor with the younger ones in the middle. The last of the 'children' died in 1942.

By the cottage is a large gallery and tea room displaying a variety of local arts and crafts including pottery, woodwork, wrought iron and paintings.

We return to Minstead by a slightly shorter route. Retrace your steps, turning right as you leave the gardens, then right again by the first sign in front of the grassy triangle to follow the lane for about 100 yards. Look carefully for a small half-hidden stile and footpath sign on your left.

❺ Turn left over the stile and walk straight ahead down a field keeping a hedge on your left. Cross the plank bridge over a stream and climb a small wooden fence to continue up the field ahead still keeping the hedge on your left. The path leads to a stile and footpath sign.

❻ Cross the stile to a road and turn right. (To visit the Honeysuckle Restaurant turn left for a few yards.) Walk down the road to the Trusty Servant inn which you will see ahead.

ROBIN HOOD COUNTRY: DENNY WOOD AND BISHOP'S DYKE

Length: 5 miles

Forest wetlands near Shatterford car park.

Starting point: Shatterford car park near Beaulieu Road Station. (GR 348 064) From Lyndhurst take the B3056, Beaulieu road. After about 4¹⁄₂ miles, just before the road crosses the railway, turn right into Shatterford car park. **Public Transport:** Alight at Beaulieu Road Station, one of the stops on that most useful line for walkers running between Southampton and Bournemouth. The car park is close to the station, to the west of the road. **Map:** Ordnance Survey Outdoor Leisure 22. **Refreshments:** Beaulieu Road Inn.

Have you ever envied Robin Hood his free and easy sort of life among forest glades? If he were to come back with his merry men he might be sad to see how little remains of his beloved Sherwood but there would be no need for him to despair. A ride south to the New Forest and he would find just the country he was used to: wide lawns and ancient oaks, tangled holly thickets sheltering the deer, quiet ways into remote valleys. He might find a shortage of rich sheriffs and

Norman knights perhaps – but apart from these minor problems he would feel at home here. This walk takes you to real Robin Hood country, the ancient oak and beech woods of Denny. And towards the end of the walk you will come across an unsolved mystery – why should a medieval bishop want a boggy patch of New Forest land?

THE WALK

❶ Several paths radiate from the car park. Ignore the obvious track which runs past a Forestry Commission barrier – that is our return route. Walk back to the large car park sign, turn left and walk between the pine trees, heading west towards the open heath. The car park is on your left. As you leave the pines, our way becomes a good track and easy to follow as it winds over the heath.

This treeless expanse of open moor may appear rather desolate on a grey day, but it is a marvellous place for seeing wildlife. The first time I came here, as a stranger in late spring, I saw a large brilliant yellow bird with jet black markings on its wings and tail flying in graceful curves over the low bushes. Another visitor told me we were watching a golden oriole. This exotic bird migrates through southern England in the spring and occasionally stops for a few days' rest in the New Forest on his way to a warmer climate.

Ahead of you a misty fringe of trees forms the outline of Denny Wood. When the path divides, follow the left-hand track. Close to the wood the path divides again. Ignore the left-hand path and keep straight on over all joining tracks into the wood.

At first you walk through groves of self-sown silver birches and it is these delicate trees that have helped the oaks and beeches they shelter to achieve their full beauty. Foresters often make deliberate use of thinned birchwoods to protect young beeches and pines from strong winds and hard frosts. Denny Wood – classified as an 'ancient and ornamental woodland' – is one of the last sanctuaries of the lesser spotted or barred woodpecker. He is smaller than the rest of the woodpecker family; only about five inches long, with distinctive bands of black and white across his back and wings which show up clearly against the tree trunks.

Follow the main path through the wood for almost 1/2 mile when it curves right to bring you to the lane to Denny Lodge.

❷ Turn left and follow the lane downhill across a lush green valley. (Ignore a track leading to a gate on your right.) You pass Denny Lodge on your right which has a weather vane surmounted by a replica of a red deer stag. He stands, head into wind, as he would in the wild. Keep straight on as the lane becomes a track and go through the gate into Denny Lodge Inclosure. We are aiming for the railway as it curves due west on its way to Brockenhurst. Follow the gravel track through the pines for about 3/4 mile past a gravel track on your left to a crosspath with a gravel track leading right.

❸ We turn left here along a green ride. (You are deep in the woods and you may have to pick your way through the grass and bracken for about 1/2 mile – but the

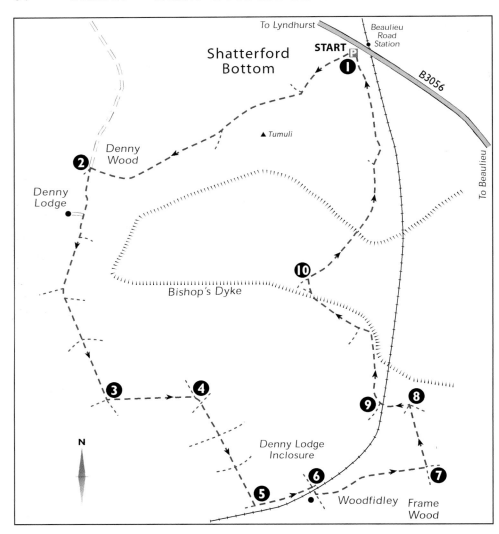

route is easy to follow.) The ride meets a T-junction.

4 Turn right and walk over a crosstrack to follow the ride to the top of a rise. Go over another crosstrack and keep straight on down the green ride ahead. This leads over a gravel track to a stile before wide lawns crossed by the railway.

5 Climb the stile and turn left to walk over the lawns with the railway on your right.

In Denny Wood.

The curves in the line earned this railway the name of *Castleman's Corkscrew*. Castleman ordered the line to be constructed in this way to avoid cutting through the great woods around Lyndhurst, including Denny. The coming of the railway in the mid 19th century aroused horror in many Forest people. Philip Klitz describes their reaction in his book Sketches of Life, Character and Scenery in the New Forest. (First published in 1850, now republished in an illustrated edition by Ann Perrett nee Klitz. Website: *www.klitzand sons.co.uk*). The most virulent objections came from the driver of the local 'neck-or-nothing', the fastest coach of its day. 'Will this rum-looking drag' he inveighed, 'with its snorting breath and smoking chimbley [sic] convey its passengers in a body safely to the place named in the advertisements, or will it scatter their bruised and blackened carcases at some place on the line, or off the line, not mentioned in the bills?'

6 Follow the line to a crossing at the foot of a tall aerial and turn right over the line. Woodfidley Cottage is on your right. Turn left and you will see two paths running roughly parallel with the railway. Take the wide right-hand path towards Frame Wood. If you look left, over the line, a few fine old beeches on the hill are all that remain of the once famous Woodfidley. Forest folk still refer to 'Woodfidley rain' when they mean rain that is likely to last some time. It would be coming from the direction of Woodfidley, from the south-east.

Go through a gate into Frame Wood Inclosure and follow the path ahead passing a grove of silver birches on your left.

7 Turn left at the first crosstrack which leads you to a gate facing the railway.

8 Go through the gate and turn left along a track which climbs to cross a bridge over the line.

9 Keep ahead for a few yards then take the right-hand of the two paths you will see ahead. (Not the path leading to a gate.) Your path runs beside the eastern boundary of Denny Lodge Inclosure. The path is embanked and runs beneath arches of fine trees including some splendid beeches, possibly more remnants of ancient Woodfidley. When the woods become more open with glades of silver birches keep straight on with the denser woodlands now on your left. Soon you will notice a low, rounded earthwork steering a rather wandering course over the heath to cross your path in places.

This forms part of the boundary of Bishop's Dyke, an area of marshy ground about a mile in length and half a mile wide, which, until quite recently, belonged to the Bishop of Winchester. John de Pontisarra, Bishop of Winchester, persuaded Edward I to let him enclose the land in 1284. The puzzle is, why should the bishop want this boggy waste, intersected with runnels and shallow pools? Was he a keen wildfowler after the best bit of snipe shooting in the area? The land could have been drier in the bishop's day and he could only have required pasture for his ponies. Naturally a Forest legend has grown up about this neglected inclosure. In ancient times, it is said, one of the prelates of Winchester was promised as much of the New Forest as he could crawl round on his hands and knees in 24 hours, the boundary to follow his route. Certainly the wavering course does suggest the route of someone proceeding with difficulty.

Continue along the main track past all turnings until you come to a T-junction where a path leads left into the woods and a grass and gravel track leads right over the open heath.

10 Turn right and follow the grass and gravel track over two bridges. The path leads you through a gap in the north-eastern embankment of Bishop's Dyke and now you will see the pines shading Shatterford car park across the heath a little to your left. The path heads north towards the pines and you enter the car park along the path I mentioned at the beginning of the walk. Walk past the Forestry Commission barrier to return to your car or train.

THE RUFUS STONE

Length: 2 miles

The Rufus Stone in Canterton Glen.

Starting point: The Rufus Stone car park. (GR 270 125) Approaching from the west turn left off the A31 Ringwood–Southampton road following the sign for the Rufus Stone. The car park is on your right. Approaching from the east take the B3079 from the Cadnam roundabout signed for Brook and turn left in the village following the sign for Stoney Cross. Drive past the Walter Tyrrell pub to the Rufus Stone car park on your left. **Public Transport:** None. **Map:** Ordnance Survey Outdoor Leisure 22. **Refreshments:** The Walter Tyrrell pub.

The New Forest, with over 900 years of history, has more than its share of secrets. On 2nd August 1100, William the Conqueror's favourite son, William Rufus, King of England, was shot dead by an arrow while hunting in Canterton Glen. The arrow was allegedly shot by a nobleman who was with him, Walter Tyrrell. An accident? Or was it murder? We visit the spot where it is believed the king fell, now marked by the Rufus Stone. Historians may differ over the facts concerning his death, and the place where he fell may not be known exactly but what is so exciting for us today is that the Forest remains much as he saw it. He would still recognise the woods and glades of Canterton Glen.

THE WALK
Before we begin our walk, cross the road from the car park to the Rufus Stone.

The Stone looks rather like an iron-encased trig point, shaped like a small tower with four sides giving an account of the king's death. According to the contemporary chroniclers, on that fateful August day the king was hunting with his younger brother Henry, his good friend Fitzhamon, and Walter Tyrrell who had just arrived from Normandy which was ruled by the king's eldest brother Duke Robert. As the sun was setting the king found himself alone with Tyrrell. A stag bounded past. 'Shoot!' cried the king after his arrow only slightly wounded it. Tyrrell shot and his arrow pierced the king's heart. He died immediately. Tyrrell fled to Normandy but no pursuit was organised. No-one even cared for the king's body. He was left where he fell to be found by a charcoal burner called Purkiss who took his body in his cart to Winchester along a route still called the King's Road. Rufus was buried without ceremony behind the altar.

Henry rushed to Winchester to seize the national treasury, then rode to London where he persuaded the Bishop to crown him king on 5th August – only three days after his brother's death! Haste was necessary as he had promised allegiance to his eldest brother, Duke Robert, in Normandy. Fitzhamon rushed to Normandy to tell Robert what had happened.

If it was murder you can take your pick from a host of suspects. The Saxons hated their Norman kings of course but even his own countrymen detested William Rufus. The clergy – rich and powerful – objected to his choice of favourites, the barons disliked him for extending his Forest laws over their lands. Then there were the allies of his brothers who had their eyes on the crown. The evidence does seem to point to Henry as the villain of the piece. Read Duncan Grinnel Milne's book The Killing of William Rufus *and see what you think!*

❶ Return to the road and cross over to the car park. On your left you will see a track and a sign 'Access to Cottage, please keep clear'. Follow the track towards the old-world cottage set in a charming garden.

In the past most New Forest cottages were built with mud walling known as 'dob'. A Forest historian, Heywood Sumner, explains how they were constructed. Clayey loam with small stones in it was mixed with heather, rushes or straw which was thoroughly puddled into the mass with tramping. This was 'dobbed' or bonded by the builder with a three-pronged fork in successive layers on stone or brick foundations. Only two feet could be raised at a time, and each layer had to be left for ten days to dry out. Finished walls were often coated with plaster or pebbledash. The cottages with their thick walls are cool in summer and warm in winter. Unfortunately, no New Forest home is proof against Walter Tyrrell's dog. According to Forest legend his ghost is able to run in and out of houses through the walls – not a happy thought at bedtime!

❷ Turn right in front of the cottage then bear left through the woods with

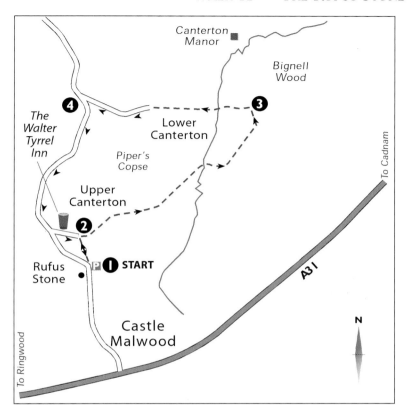

the hedge close on your left. The hedge merges into the embankment of the inclosure boundary. Keep straight on through the trees keeping the boundary a few yards away still on your left. Use the boundary as your guide as you continue over a more open area and cross a stream. Beyond the boundary which is now closer on your left, you will see the fields surrounding the tiny Forest hamlet of Lower Canterton. As you approach the hamlet the boundary is replaced by a hedge. Follow the line of the hedge as it curves left. Continue straight ahead along a gravel track with the open Forest on your right and the scattered houses of the hamlet on your left.

Dreaming peacefully beneath the shelter of the Forest oaks, Lower Canterton looks as remote as it was in the days of William Rufus. But its history is much older. After the Roman legions in Britain were recalled to Rome in AD 410 Jutish tribes were the first invaders to settle in the New Forest. They also settled in Kent. Canterton means 'the village of the Kentish men'. Later this small

A typical New Forest cottage near the Rufus Stone.

settlement must have become an isolated outpost in a predominately Saxon area.

❸ Look for a bridleway sign on your right pointing to a wide green way between the houses on your left. Turn left to follow the bridleway towards a wood, Piper's Copse. Cross a stream to walk through the wood. The track sinks between high banks entwined with tree roots and can be muddy. If so, you can follow a footpath along the top of the right-hand bank. The track brings you to a lane. Keep straight on along the lane to a road.

❹ Turn left to follow the road past the houses of Upper Canterton. Pass the Walter Tyrrell pub on the left. Continue along the road – or take the path leading from the attractive cottage – to return to the Rufus Stone and the car park.

THE NORTHERN FOREST

This is the wildest and most remote part of the Forest. You will find some old woods here – the great beeches in Bramshaw Wood can rival those in Denny – but generally the country is more open and hilly. Several streams flow south-west across the northern Forest to meet the Avon through shallow valleys. Each valley is different and provides splendid walks along the streamsides and in the bordering inclosures. For me, the most interesting is the Eyeworth valley just west of Fritham. The name 'Eyeworth' is derived from the Saxon for a wooded hill, 'Ivare', and a settlement in the valley was important enough to be mentioned in the *Domesday Book*. The valley is still the perfect site for a village but the settlement seems to have vanished! It is possible that Eyeworth was one of the Saxon villages destroyed by William the Conqueror when he declared the area part of his exclusive hunting forest.

During the 19th century the Schultze Gunpowder Works was established in the Eyeworth valley and the stream was dammed to form a large pond for cooling purposes. Today few traces of the works remain. All is peace, and the pond is home for flotillas of ducks who paddle about happily among carpets of waterlilies.

The Millersford Valley.

FRITHAM AND EYEWORTH

Length: 4½ miles

Fritham.

Starting point: Fritham car park (GR 230 140). From the Cadnam roundabout take the B3079 signed for Brook and Bramshaw. Just past the Bell Inn in Brook follow the B3078 signed for Fordingbridge. After about 1½ miles turn left for Fritham. Continue for about 1 mile then turn right for Fritham village. Pass the Royal Oak pub on your right and continue along the gravel track which bears left to Fritham car park. **Public Transport:** Buses from Southampton and Lyndhurst stop outside the Royal Oak. (This is a limited service, check times by telephoning Poole (01202) 673555.) **Map:** Ordnance Survey Outdoor Leisure 22. **Refreshments:** The Royal Oak Inn.

Fritham lies at the end of lane which leads only to Forest glades. It is a charming village – just a scattering of houses and farms overlooking a wide green grazed by animals. From the village we walk down to the Eyeworth valley with its beautiful lake. It is far too attractive to be called a pond! Our path then enters Islands Thorns Inclosure which has its own story to tell. There is a short ramble on the open heath with delightful views before we return to Fritham through another part of Islands Thorns.

THE WALK

❶ From the car park return to the metalled lane. We turn left here to walk down to the Eyeworth valley but before we do, look for a black iron postbox on the corner. When the Schultze gunpowder works flourished in Eyeworth valley the postbox was placed here to save the postman having to descend the hill. He delivered and collected letters every day except Sunday. Postage was one penny for a letter and a halfpenny for a newspaper. Follow the lane downhill and now the valley opens before you. Eyeworth pond sparkles through the trees a little to your right and a cloud of oaks and beeches clothes the hillside beyond. The lane runs down to the waterside. The scene must have been very different when the gunpowder works stood here!

A whole factory complex was built with huts for the workmen. The firm produced sporting powder used in the shooting of game, hares and rabbits. Men came to work here from as far away as Downton, Redlynch and Fordingbridge. The works were closed in 1910 when the last of the original three leases expired.

❷ Follow the lane straight ahead passing the approach to Eyeworth car park and the pond on your right and cross the stream. Continue past Eyeworth Lodge, the manager's house when the gunpowder works stood here, and keep ahead to the left of a Forestry Commission barrier to enter Islands Thorns Inclosure. Ignore more obvious paths on your right and walk straight on up a narrow path through the trees with a fenced embankment close on your left. The embankment curves very slightly

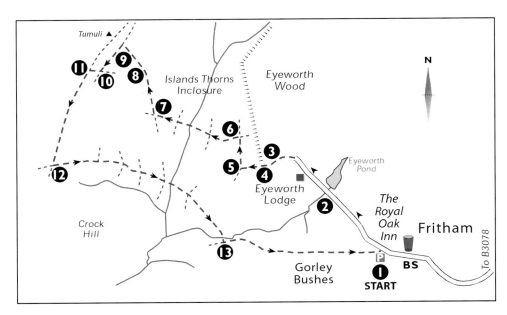

left. After about ¹/₄ mile you come to a corner where the embankment turns sharply left.

3 Leave the embankment here and walk straight ahead (your back is to the embankment). This seems unlikely as there is no path at this point but after a few yards you cross an inclosure embankment – the path is clear now leading through a dip – and you will see a wide woodland way immediately ahead.

4 Continue along this attractive path to a crosstrack.

5 Turn right to follow the track uphill. At the top of the hill you come to a crosspath by some wooden posts which once supported a gate.

6 Turn left to follow the path downhill. The path curves right leaving a large mass of fallen trees on the left to continue downhill over a crosstrack to a stream. Cross the stream and keep ahead straight over the next crosstrack. Continue walking uphill as far as a second crosstrack.

7 Turn right to follow this track still uphill to leave the inclosure and emerge on the open heath.

8 Keep straight ahead along a narrow path over the heath. You will see a line of old burial mounds marked tumuli on the map ahead of you. As you reach the mounds you come to a rather indistinct grass and gravel crosstrack. Oddly this pattern is repeated. Over the heath ahead

you will see another line of tumuli which lie beside a much clearer track.

9 This is the track we eventually follow but as there is no path to it at this point, turn left along the first crosstrack. Shortly you come to another crosstrack.

10 Turn right to walk the few yards to join the much clearer track I mentioned which ran past the further line of tumuli.

11 Turn left along this splendid track crossing the heath with the boundary of Islands Thorns Inclosure over the heath on your left. The heath rolls away to the north-west with just a glimpse of the Wiltshire Downs on the horizon. Continue, passing a grassy path on the left, for about ¹/₂ mile until you come to a wider grass and gravel track on your left.

12 Turn left to follow this track downhill to re-enter Islands Thorns Inclosure. Our way now is straight ahead along another wide embanked track. Pass a turning on your left and keep ahead past two joining tracks. On your right is Crock Hill. As the name suggests, this was once the site of a pottery. The pottery flourished in this area for possibly more than 100 years while the Romans ruled Britain.

Banks and mounds mark the site of a community of workers and while excavating here, the Forest historian, John Wise, found the remains of kilns. A typical kiln was about twelve feet in diameter and was constructed of puddled clay. Inside was the combustion chamber where wood or charcoal was burnt with the aid of suitably arranged

Eyeworth pond.

flues and an upper dome where the pottery was arranged to be fired. John Wise found parts of oil flasks, strainers, funnels, part of a lamp and even some of the workmen's tools that had been accidentally dropped into the furnace but were still recognizable. Most of the pottery he found was slate-coloured, grey or a faint yellow. You can still find fragments of bowls, platters and flagons, often decorated with a linked design. From coins found nearby it is believed the kilns ceased production about AD 380, some 30 years before the Roman legions were withdrawn from Britain.

Keep straight on over a crosstrack to cross a bridge over a stream. Go over another crosstrack and another stream to a wide gravelled T-junction.

🔞 Turn left to follow the gravelled way as it bears a little right past some fields on your left. In one of the fields you will see a mound where the gunpowder used to be stored. The track winds uphill under some magnificent pollarded oak trees to bring you back to Fritham car park.

GODSHILL INCLOSURE AND WOODGREEN

Length: 6 miles. From Woodgreen 4½ miles

The beautiful view over the Avon valley from the top of Godshill escarpment.

Starting point: Deadman Hill car park, off the B3078. (GR 193 165) From the Cadnam roundabout take the B3079. At the fork in Brook keep ahead along the B3078 and at the next fork continue along the B3078, signposted Godshill, for about three miles. Deadman Hill car park is on your right. **Public Transport:** Arriving by bus, you can join the route in Woodgreen. Your joining and leaving points are indicated in the text by bold type. **Map:** Ordnance Survey Outdoor Leisure 22. From Woodgreen: 4½ miles. **Refreshments:** The Horse and Groom pub in Woodgreen.

The western boundary of the Forest runs above the valley of the river Avon. To the north-east the Forest trees edge a steep cliff, Castle Hill, offering marvellous views over the river to the Elizabethan manor near Breamore and the farmland and downs beyond. The embankments of an Iron Age fort crown the cliff's southern corner. This walk climbs to the fort then follows the top of the cliff to enjoy the view before visiting the attractive village of Woodgreen nestling at its foot. To begin and end the walk we follow woodland ways through Godshill Inclosure.

THE WALK

❶ Deadman Hill car park overlooks the wide valley of the Millersford Brook. Across the valley, crowning the skyline to the left, is Godshill Inclosure through which our way lies. There are many paths leading downhill to the brook from the car park and it is important you find the right one. It is, unfortunately, the least obvious! As you drive into the car park look for a post indicating the Forest byelaws on your right just before you come to the circular embanked parking area. With your back to the car park, leave the post on your right and step up the embankment. You will see four possible paths.

❷ Take the one furthest left (not the path parallel with the road). Follow the path for only about 30 yards to the top of the hillside.

❸ Leave this obvious path as it descends the hillside and turn left to follow a very narrow earth path which curves left to run along the hillside. Keep to this path heading west.

❹ Shortly the path descends to bring you to a bridge with wooden handrails over the Millersford Brook. (If you have mistaken the path from the car park and find there is no bridge when you reach the stream, turn left with the stream on your right and follow the streamside path to the bridge).

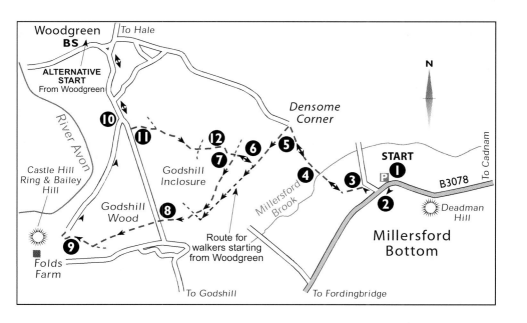

Our path to Godshill Inclosure crosses this bridge over the Millersford Brook.

Cross the bridge and climb the path ahead. As you reach the top of the hill, the path curves a little right to lead past a house and a Forestry Commission barrier to Densome Corner beside a minor road running from Hale to Woodgreen. To the left of the road is the boundary fence of Godshill Inclosure.

5 Cross to the fence and turn left to walk along the green lawns cresting the hill with the south-east edge of Godshill Inclosure on your right.

6 Continue for about ¹⁄₂ mile to a gate leading into the inclosure. Turn right through the gate and keep ahead for about 100 yards to a gravelled crossing track.

7 Turn left to follow this track through mixed woods of oak, beech, pine and sweet chestnut. When you come to a crosstrack keep straight on. **If you have started the walk at Woodgreen this is your half-way point. Turn left at the crosstrack and now follow the route of the longer walk. I will describe your route to the crosstrack at the end of the chapter.**

The track dips downhill to a gate opening to the road which crosses Godshill Inclosure from Woodgreen to Godshill.

8 Go through the gate, cross straight over the road, and enter the inclosure again through another gate. Follow the gravel track ahead. Just after a joining path on the left our track curves right and drops downhill, bearing left to a gate. Leave the inclosure through the gate to another minor road running between Godshill and Woodgreen along the top of Castle Hill.

9 Turn right beside the road for a few yards and look for a very narrow path leading steeply uphill on your left to the right of four small posts. You are scaling the side of Castle Hill Iron Age fort. Go straight over a gravel crosstrack and continue uphill to a house on the left. In front of the house bear right for a few yards, then turn left to climb the embankment and reach the smooth green lawn that forms the central area of the fort.

You are encircled by earth walls and ditches still clearly visible. This is an exciting place, full of atmosphere. It is easy to imagine the Celtic tribesmen standing here over 2,000 years ago and deciding that this sheer cliff, high above a great silver loop of the Avon, would be an ideal defensive position. They built many such forts, crowning the embankments with timber ramparts enclosing stockades with strong gates. They were an artistic as well as warlike people as their pottery and intricately-patterned jewellery prove.

Cross the central area and walk through the trees to rejoin the minor road and continue towards Woodgreen. The trees give way in front of a parking area with benches where you can sit and enjoy the view.

10 Follow the road to a junction, left for Woodgreen and right for Godshill. Turn left to see the village.

As you walk down the hill you can still see the village's famous 'Merry Trees' in the surrounding orchards. Merries are a special kind of black cherry, sweet and juicy. Once, when the fruit was ripe, people came from far and wide to pick them and enjoy what were known as 'Merry Sundays'. I read in the WI publication It Happened in Hampshire *that, in order to keep the birds from getting the fruit first, the residents used to hang tins from the branches with chains suspended inside to rattle. Ropes were attached and led through windows so they could be pulled from bed early in the morning. But the Merry Sundays evidently became a little too merry. Finally a clergyman was so shocked by the proceedings he stopped the custom.*

Join the route in Woodgreen if you have arrived by bus. From Woodgreen walk back up the Godshill Road. Pass the Castle Hill road on the right.

11 A few yards past the turning you will see a gate leading into Godshill Inclosure on your left. Turn left through the gate and follow the path ahead to meet a wider track. Keep on along this good track as it bears right. Continue over a crosstrack to a gravelled crossing path.

12 Disregard the very narrow earth path leading straight ahead from the junction and turn right along the gravel for just a few yards. Look for a green track leading left. Turn left along this track. You are

The Millersford Valley.

now back on your earlier route leading to the gate on the south-east edge of Godshill Inclosure. Go through the gate to retrace your steps along the edge of Godshill Inclosure then, bearing right in front of the house to pick up the path down the hill, cross the bridge and bear left uphill to the car park. **To complete the circle if you began the walk at Woodgreen, turn right from the gate**

leading out of Godshill Inclosure and follow the inclosure boundary along the hilltop to another gate into the inclosure. Turn left through the gate and follow the track ahead to the crosstrack I mentioned as your half-way point. Turn left as directed to follow the route of the longer walk back to Woodgreen.

WALK 15

STONEY CROSS AND BUSHY BRATLEY

Length: 6 miles

Deer in Bolderwood Sanctuary.

Starting point: Andrews Mare car park, Stoney Cross. It is closed after 6pm. (GR 255 113) From the Cadnam roundabout follow the A31 in the direction of Ringwood for about 2 miles to Stoney Cross. Turn left along the minor road signposted Emery Down and after about ¼ mile turn right following the car park sign and take the gravel track to Andrews Mare car park. Approaching from the east, there is no right turn off the A31 for the Emery Down road so continue to the Cadnam roundabout, turn right, and follow the above directions. **Public Transport:** None. **Campsites:** Ocknell (formerly Stoney Cross) and Longbeech. To get to the start of the walk from the campsites take the A31 to the Cadnam roundabout and follow the above directions. **Map:** Ordnance Survey Outdoor Leisure 22. **Refreshments:** None on the route but the New Forest Inn at Emery Down is close by.

This is one of my favourite walks. It leads you along a wide greenway dipping through heathland valleys to one of the most magical places in the Forest, the ancient oak and beech woods of Bushy Bratley. The return route passes the Deer Sanctuary at Bolderwood and the Canadian Cross, a poignant reminder of the part played by Canadian troops during the Second World War. There is so much to see and enjoy on this walk that I recommend you take a picnic and allow a whole day if you can.

THE WALK

❶ To the left of the sign 'Andrews Mare' you will see a wide green path leading west past a Forestry Commission barrier. Follow this good path which bears a little left to lead past a small pond. Continue past a larger pond

sometimes used for sailing model boats. Keep straight ahead ignoring all paths to right and left. As you head west the surrounding heathland becomes wilder and more beautiful. The path dips and rises over a shallow valley. On your left the heath slopes down to the willow-veiled marshes of Withybed Bottom. A line of trees edges the horizon. The path runs more steeply downhill to a stream, Highland Water. The stream is narrow here and usually easy to ford. Cross the stream and walk through its fringe of

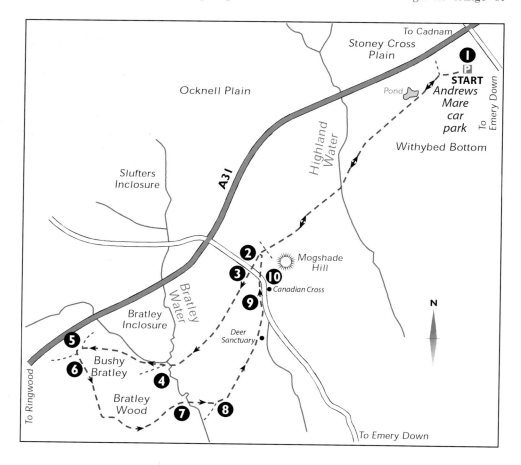

oaks and hollies to climb the hillside. As you reach the top and stand high on the heath once more, you will see the dark pines crowning Mogshade Hill ahead. Our way lies to the right of the pines, but pause here for a moment and look back. The Forest's heaths and woods roll away to the east in all their glory of colour, light and shade.

Continue along the greenway towards the pines of Mogshade to pass them on your left. Go over a small crosspath and a little further on you come to a wide green crossing path with a narrow path leading ahead through the heather.

2 Go straight over the wide path and follow the narrow path which bears very slightly left for a few yards to bring you to a minor road by cycleway signs. Over the road you will see a tempting grassy path leading south-west over the heath.

3 Cross the road to take this path which slopes gradually downhill towards Bratley Water. Beyond the stream the hillsides rise shaded with oaks which stand singly revealing all their beauty of form and colour among their green glades. An irregular verge of beech casts a heavier shadow among the surrounding ferns and heather. This is Bushy Bratley, a venerable wood even for the New Forest.

4 Cross Bratley Water, keep ahead for a few yards, then turn right to follow a grassy path with the trees concealing the stream at first on your right. The path runs along a valley where Robin Hood would have felt entirely at home! The huge trees, the wild flowers and the spicy

smells of gorse and gold withey make this an enchanted place.

No wonder Charles Kingsley chose Bushy Bratley as the setting for one of his most romantic poems. His Ballad of the New Forest *tells the true story of a keeper's daughter whose lover was a deer poacher. She warns him that one day he will be caught by her father and one evening the two men do meet, here, by Bratley Water. They fight and each kills the other. The keeper, his daughter and her lover, are buried in Lyndhurst churchyard.*

Our way winds uphill through the wood to meet the wide grass and gravel crosstrack that runs along the western fringe of Bushy Bratley.

5 Turn left along this track. Woodland slopes down on your left, a world away from the busy A31 over the heath on your right. Cross a more open area to follow the track along the edge of Bratley Wood. Keep straight ahead until you come to the point where the track curves right away from the wood to cross the heath.

6 Leave the track and turn left. Pass a path on your left and keep ahead along a grassy path heading east a few yards away from the edge of Bratley Wood. As you walk you will catch glimpses of remote heath-covered valleys through the trees on your right.

The path leaves the wood to cross a small heath to the fence along the northern edge of North Oakley Inclosure. Keep ahead with the fence on your right and cross the bridge over Bratley Water.

The Canadian Cross above Highland Water.

7 There is no path at this point but bear a little right, still keeping the fence a few yards away on your right, to meet a gravel crossing track.

8 Turn left along the track which runs uphill past the fields of Bolderwood Deer Sanctuary.

Although the Forest is home to red, fallow, roe, sika and muntjac deer it is usually only fallow who leap the fence to visit the sanctuary. You may spot an occasional black or white fallow but most have the typical 'Bambi' look – a light chestnut coat with white spots turning dark brown in winter. The deer have been coming here for food and treatment for over 40 years since the Bolderwood keeper began caring for them during a particularly severe winter. Potatoes

are their favourite food. I was told they consume over ten tons a year!

Follow the gravel track over the heath to meet the road to Emery Down. Across the road, flanked by white flag poles, you will see the Canadian Cross. Behind the Cross are two small maple trees and beyond them pine woods slope steeply down into the valley of Highland Water. The whole Forest area was used to conceal the troops and armaments massed in preparation for the D-Day landings and the pine-clad valley of Highland Water reminded the men of the 3rd Canadian Division of their homeland. The Cross was erected on the 14th April 1944 and services were held there until D-Day, 6th June. The Canadians have not been forgotten as the

Our path crossing the heath near Stoney Cross.

many tributes around the Cross testify. A yearly service is held at the Cross.

9 Turn left and walk beside the road for about 200 yards to a path on the right leading past a Forestry Commission barrier.

10 Turn right and when the path divides continue along the right-hand path with the boundary fence of Highland Water Inclosure a few yards away on your right. When the fence turns right bear a little left to rejoin your outbound route with the A31 running almost parallel along the skyline on your left. Retrace your steps to recross Highland Water and follow the wide greenway back to Andrews Mare car park.

ABOVE THE AVON VALLEY: A FOREST PANORAMA

Length: 4½ miles

The smugglers' path over Poor Man's Common.

Starting point: Hightown Common car park (National Trust), off the minor road to Hightown and Crow. (GR 181 058). Follow the A31 in the direction of Ringwood. About a mile past Picket Post turn left signposted Hightown and Crow. Continue for about ¼ mile over a cattle grid to Hightown Common car park on your right. **Public Transport:** By bus to Forest Corner, a request stop beside the A31 on the top of Poulner Hill, about a mile east of Ringwood. You have a little further to walk to join the route from the car park and I give directions for this extra distance in bold type. **Map:** Ordnance Survey Outdoor Leisure 22. **Refreshments:** None on the route but nearby Ringwood offers a wide choice of pubs, restaurants and cafés.

This is a wonderful walk with magnificent views. You really will have the Forest at your feet as you follow a smugglers' track along one of the Forest's highest ridges of moorland. West of our path Burley Iron Age hill fort overlooks the flat expanse of Cranes Moor and, to the south, wood and heaths ripple seawards to the blue shadows of the Purbeck Hills. This is a walk to enjoy throughout the year.

Before you start the walk have a look at the cylindrical concrete pillar at the far end of the parking area. This is a memorial to a remarkable man, Baron Eversley. He fought a 30-year campaign through the law courts to resist the enclosure of common lands during the latter half of the 19th century. In 1864 he launched the Footpaths and Commons Preservation Society with the aim of protecting footpaths and public rights-of-way. He purchased Hightown Common with funds subscribed by members and friends and dedicated it to the nation. We ramblers owe him a debt!

THE WALK

❶ Turn right from the parking area entrance and walk for a short distance to a track on the left signed for 'Foresters' and 'Foulford Farm'.

❷ Turn left along the track. **If you arrived by bus you join the route of the walk at this point. From the bus stop turn right over a cattle grid along a wide gravel track. Keep to the track as it curves left and shortly after bears right over Hightown Common to the minor road for Hightown and Crow. Cross the road and follow the track signed for 'Foresters' and 'Foulford Farm' which is immediately ahead.**

The track swings left past a path on the right to a Y-junction in front of a house.

❸ Take the left hand track which dips into a valley beside woods of old fir and beech. Pass the 'Hearts of Oak' works and the entrance to Foulford Farm. Continue past a Forestry Commission barrier to enter a fine oak wood, the spreading branches wreathed in ivy and blackthorn. Take either of the two paths ahead which meet just before a bridge over the Foulford stream – a much more attractive place than its name would suggest!

❹ Cross the bridge and, bearing a little left, climb the track ahead leading to the top of a high ridge. As you climb the country unfolds with spreading views. Behind is the Foulford valley with its sunny oak woods and away to the west is a glimpse of the Avon valley and the Wiltshire downs.

When I first came this way it was winter and I saw to my surprise a herd of fallow deer within a few feet of me. I had walked right past them – they had not noticed me nor I them. I counted 16, and so perfectly did their plain dun-coloured winter coats match the heathland that without their white rumps I believe I would not have seen them, close as they were. In summer most fallow deer are golden-brown, often with white spots but in winter they change to this darker shade. Fallow deer in parks can have coats of either shade but do not change in this way.

❺ As you reach flatter ground at the top of the ridge you come to the smugglers' track, a wide greenway which runs the whole length of the hillside over Poor Man's Common, where we are now standing, to Picket Post on the A31. It commands a marvellous view over all the surrounding countryside.

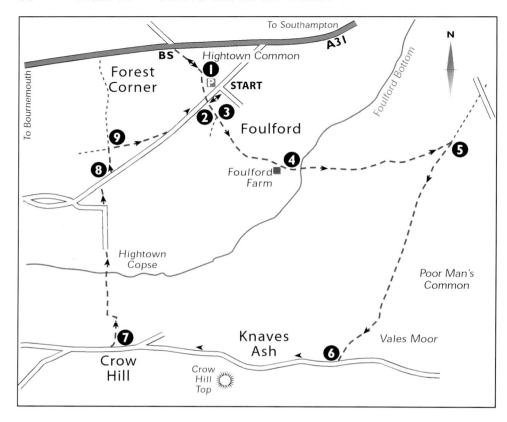

Turn right to follow this splendid path.

This ridge way was used by the smugglers to convey their contraband tea and spirits from Highcliffe, where the goods were landed, to Picket Post where, it is said, there were underground cellars for storage. A woman called Lovey Warne acted as look-out. Wearing a conspicuous red cloak she would stand on nearby Verely Hill to warn the smugglers if the Revenue men were in the area. I found it hard to believe that anyone, not wishing to be seen, should choose so lofty a route. But I believe I found the reason. A few yards to the left of the greenway, running parallel, is a deep sunken path, wide enough for men leading pack animals and deep enough to conceal people from even close observers. Have a look and see what you think!

The path falls sharply to bring you down off the ridge to the minor road that runs through Burley Street towards Ringwood and Crow.

6 Turn right and pass Knaves Ash House towards the top of Crow Hill beyond a lane on the left.

The memorial to Baron Eversley in Hightown Common car park.

Crow Hill has been a settlement since the 11th century and was once quite a busy place. Bricks were made using clay dug from a pond in autumn and trodden with bare feet in the spring. The bricks were baked in kilns heated by gorse. Gloves were also made here and one of the contributors to It Happened in Hampshire *recalls helping her mother to knit them. She was only five at the time, just old enough to knit the easy plain and purl cuffs.*

Continue beside the road for about ³/₄ mile. Look for a footpath sign indicating a grass and gravel track on the right of the road beside a small copse.

❼ Turn right along the track keeping straight on (right-hand path) at the division. Keep ahead along a narrow path bordered by tall oaks. Go round a gate into a field and turn immediately left to the corner facing woodland. Turn right to walk down the field with the woods on your left. Cross the bridge over the Foulford stream – beware the wire crossing the footway! – and follow the path bearing slightly right then uphill through Hightown Copse. Cross the stile and follow the narrow path ahead passing some houses on your right to a track. Keep ahead to a lane and carry straight on up the lane to the point where it curves left. Leave the lane here and keep ahead along the woodland footpath to a minor road.

❽ Turn right beside the road for a few yards to a track and footpath sign on

The Foulford Valley – lovelier than its name might suggest.

your left. Turn left as directed to a crossing track.

9 Bear right to walk past a mixture of modern houses and old Forest cottages to meet the Hightown and Crow road again south of the parking area just before the Forest boundary. Turn left over the cattle grid to walk over the heath beside the road, past the turning to 'Foresters' and 'Foulford Farm' now on

your right to return to the parking area and your car. **To return to the bus stop by the A31 turn left from the road opposite the turning to 'Foresters' and 'Foulford Farm' and retrace your steps along the gravel track. (You may like to make a short detour to the parking area to see the memorial to Baron Eversley before returning.) To catch the bus for Southampton, cross the road to the stop in front of the garden centre.**

THE SOUTHERN FOREST

Although this area verges on the spreading belt of coastal towns and villages it still holds woodlands and remote valleys as interesting in their own way as any in the less accessible parts of the Forest. Sir Walter Scott was reminded of his native Scotland by these southern moors. Just over what is now the southern boundary of the Forest, in the small village of Boldre where we walk, Robert Southey – once Poet Laureate – lived with his second wife, Catherine Bowles, also a poet. Both were inspired by the scenery around the village. Early in the 18th century, when wild country was considered barbarous and ugly, William Gilpin, vicar of Boldre, fostered a new appreciation of the Forest's beauty in his books. It was in the south, too, that Captain Marryat set his stirring tale of the Civil War, *The Children of the New Forest*.

Many of the Forest's wetlands remain in the south providing a wealth of interesting plants. Growing in the damp valleys you will find the aromatic bog myrtle, yellow bog asphodel and insect – trapping sundews and, if you are lucky, the rare marsh gentian and royal fern.

EXPLORING BOLDRE VILLAGE

Length: 7 miles

Boldre's 12th-century church

Starting point: Parking area close to the Filly Inn, just off the A337 on the corner of the minor road signposted to New Milton and Sway. (GR 302 002) From Lyndhurst take the A337 in the direction of Lymington. Drive through Brockenhurst and after about 1½ miles you pass the Filly Inn on your left. A few yards further on turn right along the minor road. The parking area is immediately on your left. **Public Transport:** Buses stop by the parking area. **Map:** Ordnance Survey Outdoor Leisure 22. **Refreshments:** The Filly Inn.

It is easy to miss Boldre, a quiet village, tucked away in the valley of the Lymington river, but it is a fascinating place with a wealth of stories to add to our Forest lore. You will find an ancient church where every year a special service is held which draws people from many different parts of the British Isles. You pass a house shrouded in woods, once a haunt of smugglers, and discover the legacy left by a local man rescued from pirates. Many of the houses in Boldre date from the 18th century and are restful and satisfying in their design. So you will find the village lovely to look at as well as interesting.

THE WALK

1 Turn right from the approach to the parking area and cross the A337 to the narrow lane marked with a No Through Road sign.

2 Follow the lane as it becomes gravelled and leads downhill into Roydon Woods, a nature reserve rich in wildlife. As you walk through the woods you will pass many fine trees. These include some splendid Scots pines, their flaking russet bark overlaid in patterns like wave marks on a beach.

3 When a path joins your way on the left, keep on along the main track bearing right. Pass the lodge at the gates of Roydon Manor and keep ahead as indicated by the footpath sign. The track becomes a pleasant lane bordered by oak trees, their branches contorted into weird shapes scarred and embossed to such an extent that it is easy to imagine goblin faces are peering down at you! You will not be the first to think so - the Forest is full of tales of Puck and his fellow mischievous hobgoblins. There is a wood called 'Puckpits', a heath called

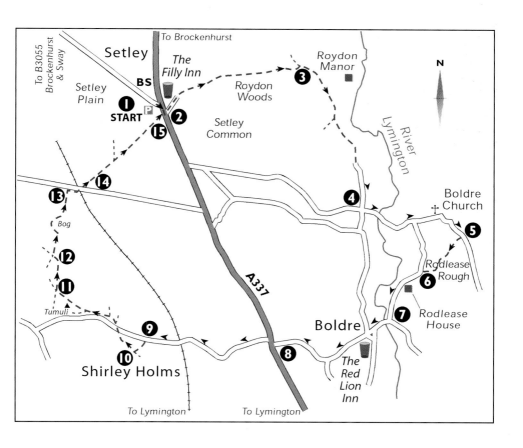

'Puckmoor', and a Bronze Age burial mound on Beaulieu Common known as 'Pixey's Cave'.

❹ When you come to a crossroads, turn left downhill for Boldre church. The lane leads to a bridge over the Lymington river. Here the river flows strongly through lush meadows dotted with dreamy-looking cattle. Willows trail long branches in the water which flows round a small island golden with kingcups in spring. Ducks quack happily in the shallows completing a picture worthy of Constable.

Follow the lane uphill to Boldre church which, like all old Forest churches, stands at the highest point overlooking the river valley.

The church of St John the Baptist at Boldre dates from the 12th century, though there was possibly an older church on the site. Its distance from the village is probably due to its original purpose, to serve as a halfway house for monks travelling to Christchurch and Beaulieu. Allow some time to look round the church as it is full of interest. There are traces of medieval wall paintings and a rare 'breeches' Bible – so called because in this edition it was considered more decorous for Adam and Eve to fashion their fig leaves into breeches rather than the usual aprons. In 1777, Boldre's most famous vicar, William Gilpin, was presented with the living and his portrait hangs in the church. At that time it was said his parishioners were little better than a set of bandits! Apart from writing his books on the 'picturesque' which made him famous, Gilpin worked hard for his parishioners, endowing a school and a house

for the poor. In 1791 he made a fascinating entry in the church register. Two weddings were solemnised about the same time. When the customary registration tax of threepence was requested, one of the bridegrooms objected. The other gallantly offered to pay for both of them, explaining his wife would not be worth having if not considered worth an additional threepence!

Boldre is known nationally as 'The Hood' church. HMS Hood, sunk in action against the German battleship Bismark in 1941, was the flagship of Vice-Admiral L E Holland who lost his life in the tragedy. He had been a regular worshipper at Boldre and his widow arranged for a memorial to be placed in the church. This includes an illuminated book of remembrance containing the names of all those who lost their lives. A commemoration service is held each year on a Sunday near the date of the sinking of HMS Hood, 24th May.

Turn left from the church entrance to continue along the lane as it curves right downhill over a stream. Climb the hill ahead and after about 100 yards look carefully for a small grass and gravel track on the right. (On my last visit the footpath sign was missing.)

❺ Turn right down the path through woodland. Just past a nursery you meet a lane.

❻ Turn left towards Boldre village past Rodlease House. During the 18th and early 19th centuries smugglers used to 'borrow' the horses out of the stables at Rodlease at night and return them in the morning with their fee – a cask or two of good French brandy!

The HMS Hood memorial in Boldre church

❼ Turn right at the next road junction to cross a fine stone five-arched bridge and walk through Boldre.

Just before you come to the Red Lion make a short detour and turn left along Boldre Lane. When I first came this way I called in at the village shop and post office. It is now a private house but you will see the red letter box still in place on the wall. I was told that the neighbouring house, with windows set in wide pointed arches, was originally a school.

The story connected with the school is fascinating. Evidently the owner of a large residence in the village, Tweed House, was unlucky enough to be captured by pirates. The villagers paid his ransom and on his return he built this little school for their children. The school is now a private house, lovingly restored by the owners who found a stone plaque recording this event in their garden. The plaque is now in the porch and reads: 'In thankful Memory of Deliverance from Brigands of the province of Salerno in Italy by payment of a Ransom of L5100 after 102 days in captivity in the year 1865 W J C Moens of Tweed Esquire erected this Church of England School AD 1869.' The story was told to me as if it all happened yesterday!

Pass the half-timbered Red Lion and climb Rope Hill past Tweed House. The name Rope Hill is a reminder of the days when rope making was a Forest industry. At the top of the hill we meet the A337.

8 Turn right beside the road for only a few yards, then turn left along the minor road, Spring Hill, signposted Shirley Holms. Follow the road under the railway bridge and you come to the Holms. Holms are hollies and just past a lane on the left our road is bordered by a most extraordinary oak wood. Each tall tree is ringed by attendant hollies which have grown long sinuous trunks spreading dark branches overhead beneath the oak tree boughs. Follow the path that runs parallel with the road through the Holms keeping the road close on your right ignoring any joining paths. You pass St Dominic's Priory on your right.

9 To see more of these immense hollies, turn left into the wood when you come to a Forestry Commission barrier. Keep straight ahead through the wood for about 50 yards.

10 Follow the path as it bears a little right to bring you to an open hillside and a crossing track. Turn right to return to the road past a car park.

We have about 1¹/₂ miles of open heathland to cross to return to our starting point. Cross the road and immediately in front of you is a Forestry Commission barrier with several paths radiating from it. Take the path furthest left which runs to the right of the road, at first almost parallel with it. Keep to the main path as it curves a little right past a joining path on the left. Continue along the path for about 60 yards when you will see a gorse-covered tumuli or burial mound about 30 yards away on your right. (The mound is thickly overgrown.) Keep ahead to a crosspath.

11 Turn right to follow the clear path heading north over the heath.

12 When the path divides take the less obvious right hand path which leads downhill round a boggy area to bring you a minor road with a railway bridge on your right.

13 Turn right under the railway to pass some wooden rails on your right.

14 Just past the rails turn left up the grass for a few steps then bear right along a mainly grassy track leading over Setley Plain. Keep to the main track over all crosstracks heading towards our starting point beside the minor road to Sway at its junction with the A337.

15 About 200 yards before the main road bear left towards the white walls and tall chimneys of the Filly Inn which you will see on the other side. The path quickly brings you back to the parking area and bus stop where we began our walk.

SWAY, SET THORNS AND HINCHESLEA

Length: 5½ miles

If you sit on this seat on the corner of Church Road in Sway, a pony will lay its head on your knee and you will never leave the Forest.

Starting point: Sway Station. (GR 276 983) Best approached via the A337 (Lymington Road) from Lyndhurst to Brockenhurst. As you approach Brockenhurst turn right signed Sway. Cross the High Street in Brockenhurst following the Sway signs. In Sway follow the signs for the station and turn left before the railway bridge to the car park. You need to buy your parking permit at the station booking office across the bridge over the line and when the office is closed you have to obtain a parking permit from the red 'Permit to Travel' machine on the platform. **Public Transport:** By train or bus. **Campsite:** Set Thorns in Set Thorns inclosure. Open all the year. There is a choice of facilities so for details tel: 0131 314 6505. Join the route of the walk at the campsite entrance as indicated in the text in bold type. **Map:** Ordnance Survey Outdoor Leisure 22. **Refreshments:** Good choice of pubs in Sway.

Sway is a large village in the south of the Forest. It is close to one of the most beautiful woods in the Forest, Set Thorns Inclosure. We ramble through the inclosure then enjoy a complete change of scene as we cross a wide valley and climb to a wooded ridge with splendid views. Our return route crosses open heathland to explore the village before leading back to the starting point of the walk.

THE WALK

❶ Walk up the lane from the station and turn left through the village. You come to a fork.

❷ Our way is left here along Mead End Road. But before you turn it is interesting to note the name of the other road, Brighton Road. This may come as a surprise but the unlikely name is due to the laying of a branch railway through the Forest in 1886. People wanted seaside holidays and when the sleepy hamlet of Bourne suddenly became the flourishing resort of Bournemouth the existing railway laid in the mid-19th century running west through the Forest to Poole was of little use to them. So a new line was laid from just south of Brockenhurst to Bournemouth with a stop at Sway. Brighton Road commemorates one of the gangs who came to help lay it. Follow Mead End Road for about ¹/₄ mile uphill.

❸ Turn right down Adlams Lane bordered by tall trees. The lane becomes gravelled and continues as a bridleway leading down to a gate opposite Set Thorns Inclosure. Go through the gate, cross the green lawn ahead and go through a gate into the inclosure. Follow the main track past a turning on the left. The track curves left and divides.

❹ Continue along the left hand track and keep straight over all crosstracks. The track heads west then curves right around Oaken Brow.

The name recalls the splendid trees that grew here early in the 18th century when, as William Gilpin records in his Remarks on Forest Scenery, *'during the unremitted course of thirty years it continued to add strength to the fleets of Britain; itself sufficient to raise a Navy'.*

Today the mighty oaks may have gone but Set Thorns still has many fine oak, beech and sweet chestnut trees. The track runs through the inclosure for about a mile to bring you to Setthorns Campsite. **Begin the walk here if you are staying on the site.**

❺ Pass a barrier and bear a little right along the gravel track leaving the campsite on your left. The track leads up to a T-junction. Turn left and cross the bridge over the disused railway (now a pleasant walk). Follow the track uphill to the site entrance, passing the reception chalet on your right. The track curves right to bring you to a minor road.

❻ Turn left and follow the road for about 100 yards to Horseshoe Bottom car park on your right.

❼ Turn right to follow the gravel approach to the car park and keep straight ahead to a barrier. Now you overlook a smooth green expanse of turf, cropped short by the Forest ponies, called Long Slade Bottom.

A 'slade' in the Forest means a valley between wooded hills. Over 200 years ago Gilpin described our view: 'A beautiful valley, about a quarter of a mile in breadth, opened before us, arrayed in vivid green, and winding two or three miles round a wood. On the other side the grounds, wild and unadorned, fall with an easy sweep

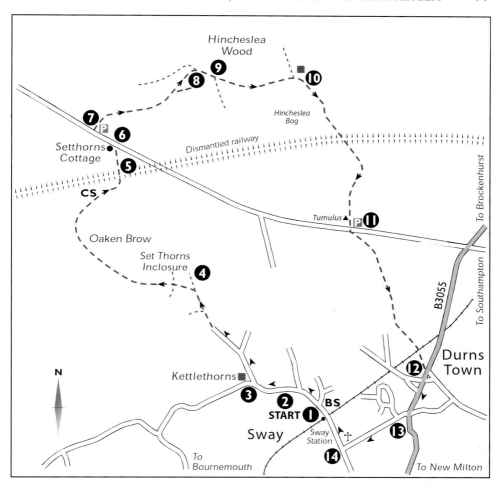

into it'. You will find the scene little changed today.

We will be making for the left-hand corner of the wood you see on the other side of Long Slade Bottom, Hincheslea Wood. Look over the green and you will see our track clearly, winding up the hillside towards the wood. Take the path

past the barrier to the green. There is no path at this point but walk over the green to pick up the path and follow it uphill as it makes its way north-east through the heather and gorse, leaving a finger of woodland on your right. As you near the top of the hill the path divides. Continue along the left-hand path until you come to a crossing path.

❽ Bear right towards Hincheslea Wood passing a grove of pine trees on your left. You come to a more open area where you need to navigate carefully!

❾ There are two paths ahead. Ignore the right-hand path which curves round the edge of the wood and keep straight on following the left-hand grassy path which leads directly into the wood. Head east along this wide way through the trees for about ³/₄ mile.

Among the trees you will see the bleached remnants of ancient oaks. In the past the oak trees in this area were specially vulnerable. Apart from their value as naval timber, their bark was used in tanning leather, a process known as 'rhining'. Sway was the centre of this Forest industry. It was said that a piece of rhine as big as a penny was worth a penny.

Keep to the main path as it dips past some old marl pits on the left. The New Forest Commoners' rights included 'the right of marl'. Marling was a method of fertilising poor land by spreading over it better material dug from pits like these. Shortly after you will see some brick buildings through the trees ahead and come to a gravelled T-junction.

❿ Turn right and follow the gravel track as it plunges steeply downhill to cross the valley. A raised causeway takes you over some of the Forest's wetlands, dotted with cotton grass and scented with bog myrtle. Shallow brooks widen into ponds fringed with tall waving

Entering Hincheslea Wood.

sedges and reeds. Continue along the track which leads between the brick sides of the former railway bridge and walk up the heath to cross Longslade View car park to the minor road. Just before the road there is a Bronze Age tumulus or burial mound on your right. Its soft green turf and sheltering gorse bushes make it an ideal place for a rest.

❶❶ From the tumulus look across the road and the heath beyond and rising above the trees you will see the top of a pencil-shaped tower.

Sway Tower, also known as Peterson's Folly, was built between 1879 and 1884 by Andrew Thomas Turton Peterson, formerly a judge of the High Court of Calcutta. It was one of the first buildings to be constructed in concrete without steel reinforcements. (According to a Forest story he received guidance from Sir Christopher Wren!) It was built by unskilled labour, 220 feet high with 12 rooms 16 feet square, one above the other, reached by a spiral staircase at the side. Why he should build such a tower is something of a mystery. Various stories circulate – one is that His Honour intended to be buried at the top and his wife at the bottom, thus showing his superiority. If this were true he was disappointed as his wife died first and his ashes were placed in her grave in Sway churchyard.

We use the tower to help us get our bearings as we cross the heath ahead. Cross the road and follow the path a little to your left which runs to the right of two short posts. The track bears a little left then curves to head directly for the tower. Keep ahead towards the tower ignoring all side tracks. When the path divides take the right-hand path still heading for the tower. The path bears a little left to leave the tower slightly to your right and you will see the houses of Sway village through the trees on the hillside. Cross the bridge over the railway and cross the common bearing a little right towards the War Memorial beside the B3055.

❶❷ When you reach the road turn right over the cattle grid to walk through Durns Town, the oldest part of Sway. Durns Town may have derived its name from the Durrant family who farmed here in the 17th and 18th centuries. Before that it was called Stamford after the brook that now flows under the road at the foot of Back Lane. You will see Back Lane on the left, just before you come to a crossroads.

❶❸ At the crossroads turn right up Church Lane. You pass Sway church on your right. At the junction with Station Road a tree overlooks a stone seat. The tree was planted in 1897 to commemorate the Diamond Jubilee of Queen Victoria. According to the inscription round the seat if you sit on it a Forest pony will come and lay his head on your knee and you will never be able to leave!

❶❹ But leave we must, so turn right along Station Road to return to our starting point. **Follow the first part of the walk from the station to return to Setthorns campsite.**

WALK 19

BY THE DARK WATER

Length: 5 miles

This wide track could be an ancient British road.

Starting point: Blackwell Common car park west of Blackfield. (GR 436 018) from Hythe drive along the A326 in the direction of Fawley. Keep straight on through Hardley then turn right following the sign for Blackfield and Lepe. Continue for about a mile then turn right at Blackfield crossroads following the road signed for Exbury. Continue over the cattle grid onto Blackwell Common and the car park is about ¹/₂ mile further on your left. **Public Transport:** From Southampton catch one of the buses that run through Dibden and Hythe to Calshot along the A326. After going through Hardley the bus turns for Lepe. After about a mile alight at the Hampshire Yeoman Inn. Walk a few yards back along the road to Blackfield crossroads. Turn left to follow the Exbury road to join the route at Blackwell Common car park. **Map:** Ordnance Survey Outdoor Leisure 22. **Refreshments:** The Bridge Tavern.

In the south of the Forest the Beaulieu river tends to steal the limelight but to the east there is a stream just as appealing in its much quieter way, the Dark Water. This remote valley was a favourite with the naturalist W.H. Hudson. He wrote about it over 70 years ago and he would find it little changed today. We follow the stream through the valley then across open heathland. Some large Bronze Age burial mounds lie across the heath on the right and I describe an optional route you can follow to visit them. We return along a wide embanked greenway which I believe to be an ancient British road.

THE WALK

❶ Turn left from the car park entrance to follow the road as it crosses the common. As you come closer to the trees of King's Copse Inclosure the road dips into the valley of the Dark Water. Cross the bridge and walk up the road ahead.

❷ Turn right into the Dark Water car park. Be sure to find the right path as you cross the car park as our way is not clear at first! Keep ahead over the gravel and bear left leaving a wooden barrier on your right. Ignore the path leading from

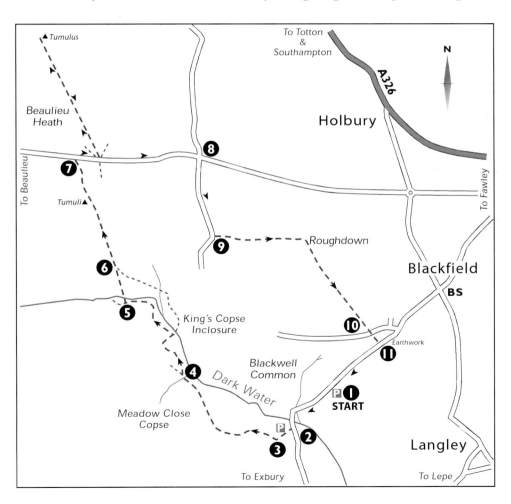

three small wooden posts, pass a large clump of bushes, then turn immediately right over the embankment to meet a good wide path.

❸ Turn right to follow this path. The inclosure fence is on your left. If this path is muddy, take the narrow path which runs beside the fence.

The path runs along the hillside west of the Dark Water through oak, holly and beech woods. The stream is invisible under its screen of willows. As the path runs deeper into King's Copse the wood becomes more remote and mysterious. Keep straight ahead through a gate. (If you are following the narrow path beside the inclosure fence, the path curves right to bring you to the gate.) Go through the gate and after a few yards the path divides.

❹ Take the narrower right-hand path which leads slightly downhill and bears left. The only sound you will hear as you follow this path through the trees is birdsong, yet Fawley Refinery is only about two miles away!

Keep to the main track past all joining tracks until you come to a crossing track. Our way curves right and downhill. The path levels and leads you to a Y-junction. Keep ahead along the right-hand path to meet a crosstrack. On the right a path leads down to a bridge over the Dark Water. We intend to follow the hillside for another $1/4$ mile so go straight over the crosstrack and follow the green path ahead. Eventually this dips downhill and curves right to a second, more secluded and attractive bridge over the Dark Water. It is still

exactly as W.H. Hudson describes it in *Hampshire Days*.

'*In this wood I sought and found the stream well named the Dark Water; here it is grown over with old ivied oaks, with brambles and briars that throw long branches from side to side, making the almost hidden current in the deep shade look black; but where the sunlight falls on it the water is the colour of old sherry from the red soil it flows over.*'

Hudson tells an amusing story about a squirrel who became crosser and crosser as he watched him. The squirrel was '*dancing about, whisking his tail, scolding in a variety of tones…and finally tearing off the loose bark with his little hands and teeth, and biting too at twigs and leaves so as to cause them to fall in showers. The little pot boils over in that way, and that's all there is to be said about it!*'

❺ Cross the bridge and climb the path ahead to meet a gravel track just before a gate on the left.

❻ Go through the gate to leave the woods behind and cross King's Copse car park to the open heath. Follow the gravel track ahead to cross the heath to a minor road.

❼ Turn right along the roadside until you come to a point where green tracks lead left and right through Forestry Commission barriers. If you would like a closer look at the Bronze Age burial mounds turn left and take the central path of the three ahead leading over the heath. This brings you to the mounds. These strange, isolated hummocks have been eroded over the centuries but there

Crossing the Dark Water.

is enough left of the largest to give some idea of the original size of the burial places of people who lived here a thousand years before the birth of Christ.

If you visited the mounds, retrace your steps to the minor road and turn left to continue the route of the walk. Otherwise just keep straight on down the road. You pass the Bridge Tavern on your right, ideally placed halfway round your walk! Continue over the Dark Water and walk up the road ahead.

If you stop and look down at the meadows on your left, you will see they appear strangely ridged and embanked and there appears to be the remains of a moat. In medieval days this was the site of Holbury Manor owned by the monks of Beaulieu Abbey. Holbury means 'a

fortress hollow' and its history can be traced back even further to Roman times when it was a flourishing settlement. And earlier still, Mesolithic and Neolithic people – from around 6,000 to 2,000 BC – hunted in the Dark Water valley. Many of their flint tools have been found here.

❽ At the top of the hill you come to a crossroads. Turn right down the gravel track following the bridleway sign leading back in the direction of King's Copse.

❾ When you come to a gate and private drive turn left to continue with trees on your right and farmland on your left. Where woods and cultivated land meet, bluebells seem to flourish. In May and June they carpet these woods, clustering thickly round the oak trees each side of the path, and spilling over into the hedges and fields.

Go through a gate and keep straight on slightly uphill to go over a crosstrack. Follow the wide greenway directly ahead.

I believe this greenway could be part of an old British track, a continuation of a recognised remnant in Fawley Inclosure. It is very wide and raised and almost all grassed over. Here and there scattered oak trees growing on the track itself form a miniature woodland walk on each side. Unlike most woodland ways, this track is well drained and determined in direction. It was probably a trading route used to bring commodities such as Cornish tin to a port near Lepe or Stone Point.

The greenway brings you to the edge of Blackwell Common to meet a minor road.

❿ Cross the road and keep straight on over the heath along the line of a low embankment marked on the map as an earthwork. Could this be all that remains at this point of the ancient road? Over the heath you come to the road between Blackfield and Exbury which we took to begin our walk.

⓫ Turn right in the direction of Exbury to return to Blackwell Common car park or left to retrace your steps to Blackfield crossroads. When you reach the main road the bus stop for Southampton is a few yards yards further on your left.

NEW FOREST MAGIC: HATCHET POND AND STUBBS WOOD

Length: 5 miles

Hatchet Pond, a favourite spot for picnics.

Starting point: Hatchet Pond car park. (GR 360 017) Leave Lyndhurst along the B3056, the Beaulieu road. Pass the turning for Beaulieu village, bear right along the B3054 for about 1$^1/_2$ miles to the junction with the B3055. Keep straight on along the B3055 for about 50 yards to the car park entrance on your left. **Public Transport:** Bus to Hatchet Gate, only a few yards away from the car park. **Map:** Ordnance Survey Outdoor Leisure 22. **Refreshments:** None on the route of the walk but Hatchet Pond is a perfect place for a picnic and there are cafés and a pub in nearby Beaulieu village.

I have placed this walk last in my Companion to the Forest because, more than any other of my rambles, it gives me the greatest pleasure. If you walk in the Forest I am sure you will agree that the Forest possesses its own quiet magic, the result perhaps of its timelessness, its peace and unassuming beauty. I feel this magical quality most strongly in the great oak woods where we find the survivors of so many centuries of our history. This walk takes you to Stubbs Wood, which, in spite of its unromantic name, is full of enchantment.

We start this walk from Hatchet Pond, a large stretch of water edged with green lawns and rich in wildlife.

The pond derives its name from 'hatch', a local word for a gateway. East of the pond the open Forest gives way to the privately-owned Beaulieu Estate. Opinions differ about the pond's origin. The Forest historian, Heywood Sumner, records that an old map of the Forest does not show the present crescent-shaped lake but on its site indicates several circles marked as 'old marl pits'. One of the commoners' rights was 'the right of marl' allowing them to dig good soil from the Forest to improve the quality of their land. The area has practically no protection from the winds that blow unchecked across Beaulieu Heath and he suggests that the action of the wind on the water which collected in the pits wore away their edges so they joined to form the pond.

THE WALK

❶ To begin the walk return to the car park entrance and turn right along the B3055.

❷ A few yards further on turn left along Furzey Lane. Follow the lane for about ³/₄ mile past a joining lane on the left which leads to a car park. When the lane forks, bear round to the left of the last house and follow the path past a Forestry Commission barrier. Ahead, several tiny streams curve round tree roots to form a watersmeet. Cross by the wooden footbridge and you will see our path leading over a Forest lawn and then uphill into Stubbs Wood.

❸ Follow the path into the wood and keep to the main path straight ahead through the trees. It is so quiet as you walk through the glades canopied by the boughs of ancient oaks you feel you should talk in whispers! All the trees have their own peculiarities. Some have fern gardens in the hollows of their branches, some appear to be sprouting out of the top of holly thickets and others have almost vanished beneath thick coils of brambles, honeysuckle and ivy.

Gradually the oaks thin and you come to a more open glade. The path is not clear at this point and to make certain you find the correct path continue for a few yards over the glade then bear a little left (not sharp left) to walk between two conspicuous holly-encircled stands of oak trees. Keep ahead, passing two more stands of oak trees on your right, aiming for the edge of a wood. The path is clearer now leading you north-west with the wood on your left and open Forest lawns on your right. Keep straight on past a joining path on your right and cross a tiny stream into Tantany Wood.

❹ Follow the clear path ahead as it winds through this beautiful oak and beech wood.

These are just the kind of trees you would expect to find in a wood called Tantany which is a colloquial version of St Anthony. The wood is dedicated to him because he is the patron saint of pigs, who every autumn are still turned out in the Forest to feast on acorns and beech mast. Once the Forest supported much larger numbers of these

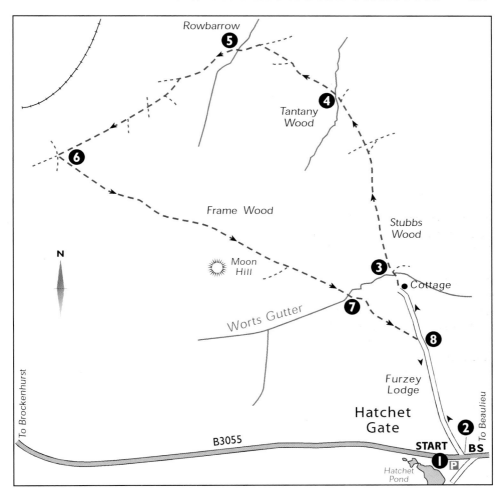

valuable animals. William Gilpin, vicar of Boldre, touring the Forest at the beginning of the 19th century, writes about the swineherd's method of introducing his animals to the Forest. 'The first step the swineherd takes is to investigate some close sheltered part of the Forest, where there is a conveniency of water and plenty of oak or beech mast ... he fixes next on some

spreading tree, round the bole of which he wattles a slight, circular fence ... covering it roughly with boughs and sods.' He gives his pigs a large supper of acorns and beech mast then 'turns them into the litter where, after a long journey and a hearty meal, they sleep deliciously'. After a few days 'they seldom wander far from home, retiring commonly, very orderly to bed'. Then he throws open the

In Stubbs Wood.

sty leaving his herd of well-behaved animals to manage by themselves.

The trees thin and a green path now winds ahead through the bracken dotted with silver birches and oaks. After about ³/₄ mile the path divides. Bear right, slightly downhill, to meet a joining track on your right. Now bear a little left to cross a small stream. (The stream may have dried up in warm weather but you will see a small ford across the stream bed.)

5 Turn almost immediately left along a broad green ride to walk beside Tantany Wood which is now on your left.

Go through the gate directly ahead and follow the gravel path into the shade of pinewoods. Follow the gravel path as it curves left and keep straight on. Ignore all side tracks and go over all crosspaths until, in about ¹/₂ mile, you come to a point where five tracks (including the one we are following) meet.

6 Our way is down the green ride on your immediate left. This soon leads you out of the pinewoods into the mixed woodlands of Frame Wood. Go through a gate and follow the path through another wood of old oaks and hollies. Keep to the main path at all divisions (the left-hand path). Through the next gate you follow a green path between pine trees. This leads to a gravel track. Keep straight on downhill to cross a bridge over a stream – named after the Old English word for plants 'Worts Gutter' – and go through a gate to leave the wood.

7 Now you have a complete change of scene. You are standing in a shallow green valley and our path winds uphill through the gorse ahead. Climb the hill following the path to join Furzey Lane.

8 Turn right to retrace your steps back to Hatchet Pond car park.

ACKNOWLEDGEMENTS

It is a pleasure to thank all the people I have met on my travels who helped me with the research for this book. I am grateful to Mrs and Mrs Hugh Pasmore who lent me books, Mr John Chapman of the Forestry Commission and the Reverend Ben Eliot and Mrs and Mrs Michael Stokes who gave me valuable information about the less-explored north of the Forest. My thanks also to the ever-helpful staff of Southampton, Totton, Hythe and Bournemouth libraries. I am grateful to Pauline Newton for her help with the first edition and Louise Burston who designed the first edition. For help and encouragement while writing this revised and updated edition I am grateful to my publisher Nicholas Battle, Paula Leigh my editor, and all my friends at Countryside Books.

Quotations from *Hampshire Days, Remarks on Forest Scenery, Rural Rides* and *It Happened in Hampshire* are by kind permission of the publishers.

Finally I thank our daughter Julie who drew the maps with so much care and my husband Mike who, while performing miracles with map and compass, managed to take the photographs as well.

BOOK LIST

John Wise *The New Forest* SR Publications First published 1883, new edition 1971.

Heywood Sumner *The New Forest* Dolphin Press First published 1924, new edition 1972.

W.H. Hudson *Hampshire Days* Barry Shurlock First published 1906, new edition 1973.

W Gilpin *Remarks on Forest Scenery* Richmond Publications First published 1791, new edition 1973.

W, Cobbett, ed C.D. and M. Cole *Rural Rides* 1930 Macdonald and Jane's.

H.E.J. Gibbens *Gypsies of the New Forest and Other Tales* 1909.

C.J. Cornish *The New Forest*

Boldre: Its Parish, Church and Inhabitants W F Perkins. 1935.

The New Forest, an Ecological History C Tubbs. 1968. David and Charles.

A Hampshire Treasury M Green. 1972 Winton Publications.

It Happened in Hampshire Published by the Hampshire Federation of Women's Institutes.

New Forest Commoners Anthory Pasmore.

British Folk Customs Christina Hole. 1976. Hutchinson.

Sketches of Life, Character and Scenery in the New Forest Philip Klitz

I have also found the Guides published by the Forestry Commission useful.

Note: *Not all the above titles are currently in print. If you can't get a particular book from your local bookseller, your local library may well have a copy which can be used for reference purposes.*